UNIVERSITY OF CAMBRIDGE
DEPARTMENT OF APPLIED ECONOMICS

MONOGRAPH 22

PROGRAMMING AND INTERREGIONAL
INPUT–OUTPUT ANALYSIS

UNIVERSITY OF CAMBRIDGE
DEPARTMENT OF APPLIED ECONOMICS

Monographs

This series consists of investigations conducted by members of the Department's staff and others working in direct collaboration with the Department.

The Department of Applied Economics assumes no responsibility for the views expressed in the Monographs published under its auspices.

The following Monographs are still in print.

PROGRAMMING AND INTERREGIONAL INPUT–OUTPUT ANALYSIS

AN APPLICATION TO THE PROBLEM OF INDUSTRIAL LOCATION IN INDIA

A. GHOSH

In collaboration with

A. CHAKRABARTI

CAMBRIDGE

AT THE UNIVERSITY PRESS

1973

Published by the Syndics of the Cambridge University Press
Bentley House, 200 Euston Road, London NW1 2DB
American Branch: 32 East 57th Street, New York, N.Y.10022

Library of Congress Catalogue Card Number: 72–76092

ISBN: 0 521 08592 6

Printed in Great Britain
at the University Printing House, Cambridge
(Brooke Crutchley, University Printer)

CONTENTS

TO THE MEMORY OF
MY MOTHER

PREFACE

In a study-cum-seminar camp organised by the Planning Commission in Nainital, India, in 1960, I presented a paper outlining some methods of studying interregional transaction flows and deriving useful conclusions on the problem of obtaining balanced regional growth with acceptable levels of efficiency in interregional production and exchange of commodities in India.

On the basis of this paper, a scheme was presented to the Planning Commission for a pilot study to explore further the problems of interregional flows and regional development. The Planning Commission was kind enough to sanction a small grant-in-aid for this purpose. A study was accordingly made of the locational efficiency of the cement industry in India. This report was submitted to the Planning Commission in September 1961 and was later published as a book.

Subsequently a more extended and comprehensive research scheme based on a multi-sectoral, multi-regional model was prepared for consideration by the Research Programme Committee of the Planning Commission. This scheme was sanctioned by the Research Programme Committee in June 1964. The work was done during the years 1964 to 1969. Much of the delay was due to the lack of good computer facilities in Calcutta.

The main report was submitted to the Commission in 1970. Since then further work has been done under the auspices of the Applied Economics Unit, Jadavpur University, extending the results into the future and studying a number of other associated problems of interest. The present publication is based partly on the results submitted to the Research Programme Committee and partly on subsequent work carried out by the Unit.

Sri A. Chakrabarty has worked continuously on the scheme, first as research assistant and subsequently as research officer. He was of great help to me in organising the vast amount of data necessary for the series of experiments. The first draft of the Appendix to Chapters 6–9 was prepared by him and has been incorporated, with some modifications in the book.

From time to time I have discussed parts of these results with Professor Ragnar Frisch of Oslo University, Professor W. Leontief of Harvard and Professor Richard Stone of Cambridge University, from whom I have received many helpful comments. Some of the results were previously published in journals in somewhat different forms.

I should like to acknowledge the support of the Research Programme Committee, Planning Commission, and their patience in permitting me to work over a period not originally conceived in the scheme. I must also acknowledge the continued support of my university and particularly of Sri P. C.V. Mallik, Registrar, in the execution of this project.

A. G.

Department of Economics
Jadavpur University

1. INTRODUCTION

This monograph is an exploratory study into the optimal pattern of regional production and exchange of commodities and the location of some important industries in India. The process of economic development in India as a whole has raised urgent problems of removing regional disparities in economic development without retarding the rate of growth. At the same time the operation of industries in the national economy must be efficient as regards production and transportation. The regional problem is of special importance to India in view of the fact that a large part of the total industrial investment currently undertaken in India is in the public sector. This investment ought to be directed particularly into the backward regions according to notions of national welfare, without however abandoning desirable norms of efficiency.

In an earlier study (Ghosh, 1965) on efficiency in location and interregional flows, the author analysed the problems of the cement industry in India. One conclusion of that study was that a more general analysis should be carried out in a multi-sector setting in order fully to understand the implications of the problem of sectoral interactions for the optimal solutions.

It was therefore necessary to choose a suitable theoretical frame for the analysis. A comparative study was made of several interregional models with special reference to the data available in India. This comparative study was useful in finally deciding on a suitable model for this work. The model selected was based on an input–output approach combined with the methods of linear programming. Both the techniques are simple and can be operated on a mass of data without too many complications. The study thus involved, at different stages, the construction of interregional input–output models and the application of linear programming to the analysis of the optimal location and flow patterns that emerge from a multi-sectoral model having fixed sectoral coefficients but no fixed pattern of regional coefficients.

This report is divided into chapters, as follows:

Chapter 2 reviews the fixed-coefficient approach to interregional problems as developed by Isard (1953), Moses (1955), Leontief (1953), Ghosh (1968) and the standard linear programming model.

In Chapter 3, empirical application of some of the above models is undertaken with Indian data and their comparative performance is evaluated.

In Chapter 4, the various linear programming models used in the experiments are described in some detail.

Chapters 5, 6, 7, 8 and 9 describe empirical exercises with the models described in Chapter 4 and include comments on their suitability and limitations.

Chapter 10 briefly discusses the dual solutions from these models and their implications.

Chapter 11 contains a discussion of some outstanding problems on which work is now being done, with particular reference to the necessity of developing more sophisticated approaches to the solution of such problems. A possible theoretical framework for using non-linear programming techniques and techniques involving variational approaches and Maximum Principle of Pontryagin are briefly developed, showing the lines along which further work is being carried out. In the appendixes the background data, are given, along with the derivation of various parameters and other information relevant to the present exercise.

SYMBOLS USED IN THE MODELS

A list of symbols used for this series of models is given below:

x_i = output if ith sector;

x_{ij} = flow of input from sector i to sector j;

y_i = final demand of ith sector for the entire economy;

$_p x_i$ = output of ith industry in pth region;

$_p x_i^s$ = output of sector in region p produced by expansion of existing installations;

$_p x_i^n$ = output of sector i in region p produced by new installations;

$_p \pi_i$ = rate of profit in ith industry in region p per unit of capital;

$_p s_i, _p s_o$ = idle capacity (slack) in ith sectors in pth region 'o' denotes 'other' sector;

$_p a_{ij}$ = Leontief technical coefficient of pth region relating sector i to j;

$_p f_i$ = final demand of the ith sector in region p;

$_p T_i$ = total transport availability in tonne-kilometres;

$_p l_i$ = labour cost of producing output worth Rupee 1 (Re) in ith industry of region p;

$_{pq} \tau$ = transport cost of varying goods worth Re 1 from region p to region q;

$_p l_t$ = labour cost of producing transport service worth Re 1;

$_p b_i$ = capital–output ratio of ith industry in region p;

$_p R_j$ = ratio of pth region's output of sector j to total output including that of sector j;

$_p k_i$ = capacity of ith industry in region p;

$_p \theta_i$ = weight of Leontief unit of ith output in region p;

$_{pq}g_j$ = constant relating regional flows with each other;

$_{pq}\tau_{ij}$ = cost of tranporting goods from sector i to j; from region p to q;

$_{pq}t_i$ = trading coefficients relating flows from region p to q to total flow from p;

$_{pq}x_i$ = flow of output of ith industry in region p to region q;

$_{pq}d$ = distance from region p to region q. Distance as used here denotes a distance between a specific centre in region p and specific centre in region q;

R = denotes aggregation of sectors within a ring structure;

T = total transport capacity of the economy;

v_j, u_i, w_i = shadow variable for dual of the transportation model;

$_p\delta_i, _pw_i$, = shadow variable of the dual of models discussed in Chapter 4; p denotes regions and i sectors, 'o' indicates 'other' sector;

$_qr_i$ = requirement of commodity produced by ith sector of all sectors in qth region;

$_p\sigma_i$ = Price index of commodity i, region p;

$_qx_{ij}$ = absorption in sector j of region q of ith product from all regions;

$_{pq}f_i$ = final demand of ith type flowing from region p to region q;

$_{pq}\kappa_i$ = ratio of input from region p to q of sector i to j in the ring.

2. INTERREGIONAL MODELS WITH FIXED COEFFICIENTS

FIXED COEFFICIENT MODELS OF ISARD AND LEONTIEF

In his pioneer work on interregional models, Isard (1953) considered the same industry in separate regions as separate industrial sectors. The analysis was then done in the standard input–output style. Moses (1955) suggested the use of trading coefficients along with the usual set of input coefficients. He defined the production function of the pth region as

$$_pa_{ij} = \sum_p {}_px_{ij}/{}_px_j. \tag{2.1}$$

He then assumed a regional coefficient, so that if $_{pq}x_i$ denotes the inflow of the ith type of goods from p to all industries in q and $_{pq}x_i$ is the total quantity of commodity i imported from all regions, we have

$$_{pq}t_i = \frac{_{pq}x_i}{\sum_p {}_{pq}x_i}. \tag{2.2}$$

We then have an assumption that if $_pa_{ij}$ is the requirement of industry of type j in region p from industry i, then of this $_pa_{ij} \cdot _{pq}t_i$ units will be coming from region p. Thus the individual inputs are replaced by the corresponding expressions $_{pq}t_i \cdot _pa_{ij}$. These are then substituted into the balance relations.

A somewhat similar formulation was presented by Leontief (1953), in which commodity was classified as national if there was a significant interregional flow of it, and as regional if there was no such flow. The regional commodities, being unrelated to flows outside the state, are taken out and solved separately. The system is described below:

$$a_{ik} = \frac{x_{ik}}{x_k}, \tag{2.3}$$

where a_{ik}, x_{ik} and x_k are the coefficient, input and output respectively, relating sector i to sector k. Regional coefficients for national industries are defined as

$$_pR_j = \frac{_px_j}{\sum_p {}_px_j}. \tag{2.4}$$

For the regionally balanced group, the equations are

$$_px_i - \sum_j {}_pa_{ij} \cdot _px_j = {}_py_i. \tag{2.5}$$

[4]

For the entire economy the equations are

$$x_i - \sum_k a_{ik} x_k = y_i. \tag{2.6}$$

Using (2.4) and (2.6) for nationally balanced goods in 2.5 and solving for the rest we get

$$_p x_i = \sum_j B_{ij} \cdot _p x_j + \sum_k C_{ik} \cdot _p y_k. \tag{2.7}$$

Regional requirements of national commodities are given by the first term on the right and regional requirements of regional commodities by the second. B_{ij}s and C_{ik}s are obtained from the basic input coefficients a_{ik} and the regional coefficients $_p R_j$.

In all these approaches a set of trading coefficients for regional flows has been assumed constant. There is no economically valid reason for assuming that inputs which are substitutes must come from one area rather than another. It is obvious that if a commodity is produced in many regions the source of supply chosen by any unit which is using it will be dictated by many circumstances, of which the most important are likely to be price, transportation facilities, time taken etc. Supplies from different regions are potential substitutes and sources of supply may shift with changing conditions.

THE LEONTIEF GRAVITY MODEL

Leontief & Strout (1963) also proposed a fixed coefficient model, for the purpose of determining regional flows. It is described as a gravity model, in the sense that the structure of the model is not unlike the usual gravity model of the physical sciences. The gravity model of Leontief is given below:

$$_{pq} x_i = \frac{\sum\limits_p {}_{pq} x_i}{\sum\limits_q {}_q x_i} \cdot {}_p x_i \cdot {}_{pq} g_i, \tag{2.8}$$

where the symbols $_{pq} x_i$, $_q x_i$ are defined as before, $_{pq} g_i$ being a constant estimated from data with respect to a base year.

The Leontief gravity model assumed that the fraction of output that region q imports as a whole is a fixed ratio of imports into q from p as a proportion of the output of p. The constant of attraction, g, is estimated through a coefficient evaluated from a set of observed values at a given period. The coefficient naturally incorporates the effect of distance, cost, and other relevant factors in regionally distributing the imports of q between other regions.

Models similar to the Leontief gravity model but defining the other variables more explicitly instead of leaving them to a coefficient evaluated empirically, were also proposed by Ghosh (1968). These analogous types of gravity models are given below:

$$_{pq}x_i = \frac{\sum_{p} {}_{pq}x_i \cdot {}_{p}x_i}{{}_{pq}d^2},$$ (2.9)

$$_{pq}x_i = \frac{\sum_{p} {}_{pq}x_i \cdot {}_{p}x_i}{{}_{pq}d^{\frac{3}{2}}}.$$ (2.10)

Here $_{pq}d$ denotes the distance of a specified point in region p from a specified point in region q, other symbols being as defined previously.

In these models distance was treated in a non-linear way. This was because it was thought that distance had more than a proportional effect on the pattern of flows. Using transport costs instead of distance was also tried out, as below:

$$_{pq}x_i = \frac{\sum_{p} {}_{pq}x_i \cdot {}_{p}x_i}{{}_{pq}T_i}.$$ (2.11)

It was discovered that the cost approach was also not sufficiently sensitive to all the implications of the transportion problem arising in long-distance flows. Long-distance transportation is not simply more expensive, it is also uncertain and time-consuming and knowledge concerning it is imperfect. The cost of transportation generally provides a poor estimate of all these various factors.

Finally, several types of regression models were tried out. The main model is described below:

$$_{pq}x_i = (\sum_{p} {}_{pq}x_i)^{\alpha} \, ({}_{p}x_i)^{\beta} \cdot ({}_{pq}d)^{\gamma}.$$ (2.12)

This regression model was tried out for the country as a whole and also separately for specific regions. The parameters α, β γ were evaluated from a regional cross-section of a single set of observations corresponding to the same period.

The common feature of all the models described above is that they are of the fixed coefficient type. The coefficients which are found once are perpetuated, even though the basic supply sources and demand centres may have changed considerably. This rigid approach to regional flow problems is unrealistic, particularly in a developing area. Regional flows are certainly sensitive to cost, distance, and transportation factors, and in a changing industrial structure this is even more important. It is necessary therefore to bring forth the substitution aspect explicitly and more definitely in both theory and application.

Keeping in mind the limitations of the approach so far suggested, a model was proposed by Ghosh (1968) in which the possibilities of substituting one region for another, or one input for another, are given full play. Sectoral and regional substitutions are treated here not as two distinct phenomena, but as aspects of the general problem of substitution itself.

In introducing this new concept, it is useful to start with the concept of the ring structure introduced by Frisch (1957). The concept of ring structure is easily explained by an example. Let us assume that there are two sectors, supplying coal and oil respectively. Let us further assume that coal and oil are available in both regions A and B, in a system containing, let us say, regions A, B, and C. An industry in region C, let us say, has a specific requirement of energy which may be supplied by either coal or oil, or both.

If one used a model with a large number of industrial sectors only for a short period, then one might assume that a particular sector had a well-defined energy coefficient which was a fraction of its total products in a suitable unit. In such a case a fairly well-defined energy coefficient might not be unrealistic. But one cannot go on from that to assume that the demand for each specific kind of energy is also rigidly fixed. In fact the essential problem is often that of choosing the cheapest of a variety of energy sources. Thus an industry may well have to choose between imported oil, domestic hydro-electric power, coal and atomic energy. It would be unrealistic to lump them all together in a single sector called energy production. These sources should be considered separately. But if these energy sectors are separately treated it will be absurd to assume that each sector needs a fixed quantity of each specific type of energy. While it is realistic to assume that the total energy requirement is a fixed constant, it would be unrealistic to divide it up into fixed requirements of each specific type of energy.

Similar considerations apply to many other types of deliveries to production sectors. Sometimes it may, for instance, be a question of replacing one kind of raw material by another, or of replacing a certain item of complementary import by a similar kind of product from the domestic sector, even though it may not be equally satisfactory.

If a certain sector, say j, requires a certain kind of input, such as energy, it need not be assumed that a particular sector is supplying this input to j, but rather that there may be a 'ring' of other sectors or other delivering categories, such as $i + 1$, $i + 2$, etc., from which the supply may come. We shall assume that the individual sectors within the ring are equivalent, in the sense that a specific quantity of the input from one of these sectors can replace a certain fixed quantity of the input from one of the other delivering categories in the ring. We also assume that sector j has a technologically well-defined requirement of this 'ring' product as a whole, rather than a separate demand for each of the components of the ring.

We shall formulate the rule for substitution of one regional source by another in the model with reference to a base period configuration with changing prices. The price data will be exogenously fed into the system, just as the final demand is usually supplied. This obviously means that for our purpose changes in the price system in the short period will be taken to be the factor determining changes in the regional pattern of distribution.

In the base period, let $_{pq}x_{ij}$ denote the flow of a specific input from region p to q and from sector i to j.

Let there be a ring structure in Frisch's sense, the ring being defined for regions from $p_1...p_r$. Thus let there be a production coefficient defined for the ring including $p_1 ... p_r$, from any one of which the technical requirement may be met.

Then the inputs in the ring are given by

$$\sum_{R} {_{p_r q}}x_{ij}, \tag{2.13}$$

where all flows from regions $p_1...p_r$ forming the ring are summed, R denoting a summation over $p_1...p_r$.

The production functions for the structure of the ring as a whole are defined as

$$R \cdot {_q}a_{ij} = \frac{\sum_{p_r q} x_{ij}}{{_q}x_j}. \tag{2.14}$$

Further, let $_p\lambda_i$ denote the price index of the ith commodity in the pth region. Let us define the index in the sense of Paasche, that is, we take the period 1 as the base and the period 0 as the reference period for which the index is being calculated. The price index in our sense is defined as follows:

$$_p\sigma_i = \frac{\text{Price of commodity } i \text{ in region } p \text{ in base period } 0.}{\text{Price of commodity } i \text{ in region } p \text{ in current period } 1}. \tag{2.15}$$

In the base period (0) let us define $_{pq}\kappa_{ij}$ as the ratio of the input of commodity i from region p going to industry j in region q such that:

$$_{pq}\kappa_{ij} = \frac{_{pq}x_{ij}}{\sum_{R} {_{p_r q}}x_{ij}}. \tag{2.16}$$

Let $_R\lambda_i$ be the mean of the price indexes defined in 2.15 for the ring with weights given by the corresponding k, such that $_R\lambda_i$ is given by

$$_R\sigma_i = \sum_{R} {_{p_r q}}\kappa_{ij} \cdot {_{p_r}}\sigma_i. \tag{2.17}$$

The base period coefficient for any region in the model is related to the ring coefficient as below:

$$\frac{_{pq}x_{ij}^0}{_{q}x_j^0} = R_{\cdot\,q}a_{ij} - _{pq}\kappa_{ij}. \qquad (2.18)$$

Then the expression we suggest for the reference period for the same region is given by:

$$\frac{_{pq}\hat{x}_{ij}}{_{q}\hat{x}_j} = R_{\cdot\,q}a_{ij} \cdot _{pq}\kappa_{ij} \cdot \frac{_{p}\sigma_i}{_{R}\sigma_i}. \qquad (2.19)$$

It should be noted that if there is no price change for the current period the above expression reduces to (2.18). This means that so long as there is no relative price change there will be no change in the situation with regard to the regional flows.

If there is a change in relative prices, there will also be changes in the coefficient structure. In the case of such changes the component flowing in from a region, or from a sector, to a particular region will decrease if the ratio of the relative price index to the average increases and will increase if this price ratio decreases.

It should be noted that the change in a particular flow may be a sectoral substitution, or a regional substitution, or both. There is no distinction between the two in the model. Thus the amount of coal transferred from region A to C may have declined because there has been a substitution of oil from A, or of coal from B, or of oil from B.

Summing over the regions in the ring, which are all parts of the ring structure, we get:

$$\frac{\sum\limits_{R} {}_{pr\,q}\hat{x}_{ij}}{_{q}\hat{x}_j} = \frac{R_{\cdot\,q}a_{ij}}{_{R}\sigma_i} \cdot _{R}\sum {}_{pr\,q}\kappa_{ij} \cdot _{p}\sigma_i. \qquad (2.20)$$

$$= R_{\cdot\,q}a_{ij}.$$

This satisfies the basic equation for the ring over the regions inside the ring.

Introduction of the parameter involving the price constellation, of course, requires more information to be supplied to the model before a solution can be had. It should be pointed out, however, that what one can do here is to project relative price ratios while projecting the final demand vector and find out the different patterns for alternative price constellations.

LINEAR PROGRAMMING MODEL

In the price model discussed above coefficients are allowed to change because of changes in relative prices. But a region is not allowed to take supplies from another region if it was not taking the commodity originally. Similarly it cannot give up importing from a region, whatever the price change. The model thus cannot consider the entry or exit of units.

The form for a logically complete substitution model is given by linear programming. The usual programming model for this purpose may be formulated as follows:

Given the production functions for the sectors,

$$\sum_{p} {}_{pq}x_{ij} = {}_{q}a_{ij} \cdot {}_{q}x_{j}, \tag{2.21}$$

and given the balance relations for the regions,

$$\sum_{q} \sum_{j} {}_{pq}x_{ij} + \sum_{q} {}_{pq}f_{i} = {}_{p}x_{i}, \tag{2.22}$$

$$\sum_{p} \sum_{j} {}_{pq}x_{ij} + \sum_{p} {}_{pq}f_{i} = {}_{q}r_{i}, \tag{2.23}$$

the objective is to find a set of flows which will minimise the total transport costs, given by

$$\sum_{p} \sum_{q} \sum_{i} \sum_{j} {}_{pq}a_{ij} \cdot {}_{pq}x_{ij}. \tag{2.24}$$

3. THE APPLICATION OF FIXED
COEFFICIENT MODELS

A set of models has been formulated in the previous chapter, mainly of the fixed coefficient type, some of them determined mainly by past patterns of outputs and flows and some influenced also by prices. The last model formulated is based on linear programming. In the following sections empirical demonstrations are given of these models, in order to evaluate their comparative performance.

Before presenting the results, it may be useful to give a brief description of the data for the experiment. The data relate to the flow of cement into various importing regions in India from different producing regions in the four years 1950, 1954, 1957 and 1959. The regions in question consist of separate states where these are large, otherwise the states have been grouped together.

The fixed coefficient model of Isard has been defined in (2.1) and (2.2). The inflows into regions in the model are strictly proportional to the total inputs of the consuming regions. The Leontief model as defined in (2.3)–(2.7) is also of a similar type analytically, except that it treats the sectors in two distinct clusters, one of which can be determined separately and independently before the other has been determined. Table 3.1 gives the observed and computed values of the Isard model averaged for the years 1950, 1954 and 1957.

TABLE 3.1. *Flow of cement in 1000 maunds†   averaged over 1950, 1954 and 1957 as observed and as computed by the Isard model*

| | To West Bengal‡ | | To Uttar Pradesh‡ | |
From	Observed	Computed	Observed	Computed
West Bengal	0	0	2	317
Bihar	8200	9170	640	731
Orissa	1183	41	0	1
Uttar Pradesh	1	19	0	0
Punjab	16	19	1733	4123
Bombay	1	0	61	123
Madras	127	0	3	1
Rajasthan	1	14	4723	2110
Hydrabad	0	0	0	0

† 1 maund = 37.32 kg.   ‡ These four states are the major importers.

T A B L E 3.1. (*cont.*)

From	To Punjab‡		To Bombay‡	
	Observed	Computed	Observed	Computed
West Bengal	2	243	1	0
Bihar	39	112	3	0
Orissa	399	9	0	0
Uttar Pradesh	15	3	1	0
Punjab	0	0	321	740
Bombay	62	532	0	0
Madras	206	5921	108	159
Rajasthan	6868	2614	555	1398
Hydrabad	1642	0	3427	1320

T A B L E 3.2. *Flow of cement in 1000 maunds averaged over 1950, 1954 and 1957 as observed and computed by Leontief's gravity model*

From	To West Bengal		To Uttar Pradesh	
	Observed	Computed	Observed	Computed
West Bengal	0	0	4	88
Bihar	2800	8019	674	506
Orissa	1019	1124	0	33
Uttar Pradesh	1	11	0	0
Punjab	16	51	1439	1156
Bombay	1	0	29	102
Madras	129	0	92	1
Rajasthan	1	27	4850	4187
Hydrabad	0	0	0	3

From	To Punjab		To Bombay	
	Observed	Computed	Observed	Computed
West Bengal	2	18	1	0
Bihar	39	97	3	0
Orissa	399	308	0	0
Uttar Pradesh	11	1	1	12
Punjab	0	0	321	363
Bombay	68	500	0	0
Madras	262	3944	108	83
Rajasthan	7065	5637	554	3199
Hydrabad	1642	0	3427	79

It may be seen that Isard's model, starting as it does with a rigid initial production situation, fails to respond to changes. When new industries come up in regions where there were no such industries previously, the situation changes very drastically in reality, but this is not reflected by the model.

THE LEONTIEF MODEL

Table 3.2 gives a numerical demonstration of the Leontief gravity model (2.8). Table 3.3 demonstrates the variant suggested by us in (2.9) and in (2.10). Some states are not presented because the demonstration was a complete failure in those cases.

TABLE 3.3. *Flow of cement in 1000 maunds averaged over 1950, 1954 and 1957 as observed and computed by the alternative formulation of the gravity model*

From	To West Bengal		To Uttar Pradesh	
	Observed	Computed	Observed	Computed
West Bengal	1	0	56	18
Bihar	9979	6983	607	1953
Orissa	770	524	0.5	174
Uttar Pradesh	3	6	1.5	0
Punjab	39	169	1794	2043
Bombay	0.5	19	42	69
Madras	95	96	69	110
Rajasthan	2.5	458	4000	3502
Hydrabad	0	162	0.3	0

From	To Punjab		To Bombay	
	Observed	Computed	Observed	Computed
West Bengal	9	9	1	59
Bihar	32	526	2	137
Orissa	300	60	0	92
Uttar Pradesh	9	28	8	10
Punjab	0	0	696	606
Bombay	65	36	0	0
Madras	355	43	108	328
Rajasthan	5369	6530	873	2141
Hydrabad	1230	116	2286	368

From these results it can be seen that while they generally do better than the fixed coefficient model, the gravity models are not able to reflect the impact of change in a realistic manner. An area, however far from the centre of consumption, still remains a significant centre of supply if only it is big enough. This may be acceptable as long as adjacent centres of supply do not operate but is bound to fail when such centres are developing.

The third set of models tried out was of the regression type, where a function was fitted involving both distance and volume of production, with data of a regional cross-section type.

The equations fitted were as follows:

$$\text{Indian Union} \quad {}_{pq}x_i = {}_px_i^{1.4531}d^{-1.8911}\left(\sum_p {}_{pq}x_i\right)^{0.5463}, \qquad (3.1)$$

$$\text{Uttar Pradesh} \quad {}_{pq}x_i = d^{-0.9143}\left(\sum_p {}_{pq}x_i\right)^{1.3839}, \qquad (3.2)$$

$$\text{Bombay} \quad {}_{pq}x_i = d^{-1.0491}\left(\sum_p {}_{pq}x_i\right)^{1.4724}. \qquad (3.3)$$

Table 3.4 gives results for only two regions, Uttar Pradesh and Bombay. The other two regions had to be dropped because of poor performance.

TABLE 3.4. *Flow of cement in 1000 maunds averaged over 1950, 1954 and 1957, as observed and computed by the regression model*

From	To Uttar Pradesh		To Bombay	
	Observed	Computed	Observed	Computed
West Bengal	2	1	1	0
Bihar	641	597	3	495
Orissa	0	64	0	31
Uttar Pradesh	0	0	1	0
Punjab	1683	286	320	81
Bombay	29	15	0	0
Madras	92	56	108	65
Rajasthan	5186	1837	555	1215
Hydrabad	0	167	3427	343

The model was fitted for India by averaging the supply conditions and volumes of supply in different regions of the Indian Union. The model failed because of the great disparities between the regions. As may be seen, the curves fitted separately for the regions are also not very successful. A better procedure, of course, would have been to fit for each region separately over different time periods. But the data for such fitting were not available.

TABLE 3.5. *Flow of cement in 1000 maunds averaged over 1950, 1954, and 1957 as observed and computed by the price substitution model*

From	To West Bengal		To Uttar Pradesh	
	Observed	Computed	Observed	Computed
West Bengal	0	0	6	201
Bihar	7110	7276	913	887
Orissa	793	549	0	1
Uttar Pradesh	2	6.5	0	0
Punjab	24	106	1286	2847
Bombay	0	1.5	26	72
Madras	190	191	139	116
Rajasthan	0	6	3442	2680
Hydrabad	0	0	0	1

From	To Punjab		To Bombay	
	Observed	Computed	Observed	Computed
West Bengal	2	68	0	0
Bihar	53	132	1	0
Orissa	307	147	0	0
Uttar Pradesh	12	20	2	6
Punjab	0	0	465	943
Bombay	52	204	0	0
Madras	109	2100	150	162
Rajasthan	6242	3184	309	714
Hydrabad	1760	2624	1948	1058

SUBSTITUTION MODELS

The results for the price substitution model with varying coefficients, which was discussed in (2.17), are given in Table 3.5.

The kind of price index used is not a sufficiently sensitive instrument for forecasting changes in the regional flows in this area. If a suitable indicator could be found of the changing prices at which different amounts of supplies are made available, it would be a better variable for explaining the change in the pattern of regional flows. Models of this type may work better in a more stable economic situation, where more or less unlimited amounts may be supplied at certain prices in the various regions. But in an area where capacities are limited and new industries are growing, capacity bounds are changing all the time and such models are not adequate to describe the drastic changes continuously taking place.

THE LINEAR PROGRAMMING MODEL

Table 3.6 gives a demonstration of the programming model, under conditions similar to those discussed in relation to the fixed-coefficient type of models.

TABLE 3.6. *Flow of cement in 1000 maunds averaged over 1950, 1954, 1957 and 1959 as observed and computed for the programming model*

From	To West Bengal		To Uttar Pradesh	
	Observed	Computed	Observed	Computed
West Bengal	0	0	56	0
Bihar	7479	7787	607	836
Orissa	893	514	—	366
Uttar Pradesh	3	0	0	0
Punjab	39	0	1794	2454
Bombay	6	0	40	525
Madras	95	0	69	100
Rajasthan	3	0	4251	2542
Hydrabad	0	0	—	0

From	To Punjab		To Bombay	
	Observed	Computed	Observed	Computed
West Bengal	8	0	1	0
Bihar	32	0	2	88
Orissa	300	0	0	0
Uttar Pradesh	9	20	8	14
Punjab	0	0	646	7
Bombay	65	0	0	0
Madras	330	0	109	210
Rajasthan	5376	7378	873	638
Hydrabad	1231	0	2937	3669

— Indicates insignificant amounts.

The programming model does take into account the fact that capacities and requirements are changing all the time. It takes each such situation as a discrete situation and in this respect it is realistic. Where it is not realistic is in the precise measurement of cost. Further, to the extent that competitive conditions do not exist, the observed and computed costs may diverge. Part of the deviation from actual costs is due to lack of precision in measurement of distance and cost and part is due to lack of competitive conditions.

COMPARATIVE PERFORMANCE

In Table 3.7 an analysis of the relative performance of these models is given by presenting the total absolute deviation of actual from computed results by the different methods. Generally, however, it may be noted that the programming model gives a better approximation to reality than the other models, in spite of the limitations pointed out above.

TABLE 3.7. *Total deviation from observed values in 1000 maunds (absolute values)*

Year	Region	Isard	Leontief gravity (1)	Alternative gravity (2)	Price model	Regression	Programming	Actual
1950	West Bengal			1027			308	5471
	Uttar Pradesh			1600			4358	5123
	Punjab			1336			1466	1013
	Bombay			3759			3668	3269
1954	West Bengal	2524	2483	1476	2539		974	8687
	Uttar Pradesh	4514	5102	2871	4738	5119	4439	7266
	Punjab	7764	5942	4890	7976		5656	5700
	Bombay	800	2331	2639	1475	2358	3411	2712
1957	West Bengal	1761	1574	1753	1614		984	7553
	Uttar Pradesh	5898	1069	2546	2991	3132	3933	5337
	Punjab	15 529	7296	2701	9741		3301	11 286
	Bombay	3553	5647	5422	3327	4440	301	3042
1959	West Bengal	2865	1884	2885			1931	11 876
	Uttar Pradesh	9965	3434	4641		6994	3922	9566
	Punjab	15 066	8983	4488		7340	5346	11 394
	Bombay	8577	11 314	11 228			2218	7493

4. LINEAR PROGRAMMING MODELS

THE GENERAL FRAMEWORK

It was noted in the previous chapter than the fixed coefficient models for regional flows often failed to reflect the fast-changing character of the regional supply and demand situation in India. It was also noted that the programming model gives a more satisfactory description of the flow, as it takes into account this change in the character of regional demand and supply over time. It was therefore concluded that for a study of interregional flows, linear programming models are better descriptions of reality. They have an additional advantage, in that they show a way towards achieving optimal patterns. In subsequent chapters, therefore, the linear programming model is made the main basis for our series of experiments. In the following sections the theoretical framework for the models used in these experiments with Indian data are discussed in some detail.

The main approach in these models is a combination of programming techniques and those of input–output analysis. All the models used in this experiment have a basically similar framework. It may therefore be useful to discuss the bare essentials of the common framework for this group of models.

THE CONSTRAINT SYSTEM

The model assumes that production coefficients are different for different regions and that regional flows are determined subject to certain objectives for the regions as a whole.

The balance relation for a specific row indicates that all inter-industrial flows into other regions over all sectors and all final demand flows are equal to the requirement of the sector in the region.

The balance relation is written as

$$\sum_{p} \sum_{j} {}_{pq}x_{ij} + \sum_{p} {}_{pq}f_i = {}_{q}r_i. \qquad (4.1)$$

This balance relation relates to inputs from all regions to a specific region.

Introducing Leontief coefficients for regions, we have

$$\sum_{p} {}_{pq}x_{ij} = {}_{q}a_{ij} \cdot {}_{q}x_{j}. \qquad (4.2)$$

We thus define the input coefficient for a sector in any region irrespective of the various sources from which the inputs may come. The inputs are thus aggregated over all sources.

[18]

Rewriting the balance equation (4.1), we have

$$\sum_j {}_qa_{ij} \cdot {}_qx_j + \sum_p {}_{pq}f_i = {}_qr_i. \qquad (4.3)$$

This is a formal statement of the accounting or balance relation, including the technical coefficients. This has to be slightly modified as data on interregional flows are not generally available separately for each importing sector, but only for all sectors of a region together. The balance relation was therefore written by aggregating the supply sources, as below

$$\sum_j {}_qx_{ij} - \sum_p {}_{pq}x_i + \sum_p {}_{qp}x_i + {}_qf_i = {}_qx_i. \qquad (4.4)$$

This means that the inter-industrial absorption in the qth region, less deliveries from all regions to the qth region, plus exports from q to other regions plus final demand of qth region must equal home production of the qth region. The absorption by industries in the qth region is thus aggregated over all supplying regions including itself.

Rewriting this balance relation, using the technical coefficients for all regions irrespective of the origin of the inputs, we have

$$\sum_j {}_qa_{ij} \cdot {}_qx_j - \sum_p {}_{pq}x_i + \sum_p {}_{qp}x_i + {}_qf_i = {}_qx_i. \qquad (4.5)$$

As before, symbols pq and qp denote the directions from p to q and from q to p respectively.

With separate regional input–output tables showing flows from all regions to any particular region one can now obtain a set of equations relating the inputs, outputs, exports and imports of a group of industries together. This is the common accounting framework for the model. In this case, the balance relates, of course, to a group of industries rather than the economy as a whole.

Apart from the balance relation considered above we have also several constraints defined by capacity limitations in different sectors. These capacity limits are generally assigned from *a priori* knowledge. With these capacity limits and balance equations as constraints we shall consider three broad types of objectives for the optimal problem.

The first set of objective functions seeks to minimise the total labour and transport costs of production in the sectors which are in the model. The importance of labour minimisation in this problem arises from the fact that the industries selected are such that skilled labour for such industries is a scarce factor and should be used optimally. In another set of problems transport has also been treated as a separate sector with respect to the intermediate consumption of transport. The movement of commodities to the final consumers and the associated transport requirements have been considered explicitly in the model.

THE MODELS MINIMISING LABOUR AND TRANSPORT COSTS

Model 1

Minimise,

$$\sum_p \sum_i {}_p l_i \cdot {}_p x_i + \sum_p \sum_q \sum_i {}_{pq} x_i \cdot {}_{pq} \tau_i, \tag{4.6}$$

subject to

$$(1 - a_{ii})\, {}_p x_i - \sum_j {}_p a_{ij} \cdot {}_p x_j - \sum_q {}_{pq} x_i + \sum_q {}_{qp} x_i = {}_p f_i, \tag{4.7}$$

$$\sum_p \sum_q \sum_i \left({}_{pq} x_i\right) \left({}_{pq} d\right) \left({}_p w_i\right) \leqq \sum_p \sum_q {}_{pq} T, \tag{4.8}$$

$${}_p x_i \leqq {}_p \bar{x}_i, \tag{4.9}$$

$i, j = 1, \ldots, 4 \text{ industries}$

$p, q = 1, \ldots, 6 \text{ regions}$

${}_p \bar{x}_i$ is the assigned capacity limit.

Equation (4.7) is the familiar accounting or balance relation discussed above. Equation (4.8) gives the transport constraint for the problem. This was framed in the following way:

Let a unit of material (worth a fixed value of money) of any type i be associated with actual weight w_i, so that $w_i x_i$ denotes the physical weight of x_i units in this sense. Then the model requires that balance be kept between the transport availability from region p to q and the total material transported, as in equation (4.8) where $\Sigma\Sigma_{pq} T$ is the maximum weight that could be transported from p to q with existing transport facilities. It is assumed that $\Sigma\Sigma_{pq} T$ is exogenously assigned.

Equation (4.4) gives the capacity limits assigned to sectoral outputs. The objective function (4.1) seeks to minimise the labour costs of production and the cost of of transportation, subject to satisfying conditions (4.2)–(4.4).

In model 1 we consider transport as an exogenous sector. In model 2 transport is treated as endogenous. This is done in order to generalise the structure of the model and to bring in the interaction between transport and other sectors. The model is now reformulated as follows:

Model 2

Minimise

$$\sum_p \sum_i {}_p l_i \cdot {}_p x_i, \tag{4.10}$$

subject to

$$\sum_p {}_p x_i - \sum_p a_{ii}\, {}_p x_i - \sum_p \sum_j a_{ij}\, {}_p x_j = \sum_p {}_p f_i, \tag{4.11}$$

$${}_p x_i \leqq {}_p \bar{x}_i, \tag{4.12}$$

i and j now include transport as a sector.

The model considers the balance relation for the economy as a whole rather than for specific regions, though the capacity restraints are still regionally defined. The objective function now attributes labout costs to all sectors, including transport, and seeks to minimise such labour costs for the total economy.

It is generally appreciated, however, that minimisation of current labour costs is not always the short-run objective of a developing country. More efficient utilization of capital, which is generally acutely scarce, may be a worthwhile objective in the immediate or near future in order that rapid growth may be achieved in the short run.

MODELS MINIMISING CAPITAL COST

The second group of models has the same balance and capacity constraints as before, but the objective is to minimise capital use in the economy. The concept of capital used in the model is of interest and will be discussed in some detail. Broadly, in this class of models one can work either with incremental capital (new investments) or with total capital. In any economy installed capital cannot usually be shifted from one sector to another or from one region to another. Therefore one group of opinion favours the use of incremental or new capital. This new capital may be used for the expansion of an existing unit or for a completely new installation. Some of our experiments were done with the incremental capital concepts, as explained above. It is felt, however, that the incremental capital approach may have some undesirable features, especially if optimisation is being considered over a planning period of several years.

There are two types of capital, that already installed and that to be newly constructed. In some models there are two periods – an initial and a terminal period. Assuming that new constructions are required to meet new demands, such new construction is generally undertaken in order to meet the demand over a period, rather than a single point of time. Hence all such capital will have spare capacity for part of the time which will be gradually used up. If we are considering the best use of capital over a period rather than at a specific point of time, because of this surplus capacity problem the proper way will be to consider the best utilisation of the entire amount of capital installed, rather than the capital installed at a particular point of time.

The inclusion of only the new capital in the objective function may eventually lead to a higher use of capital per unit of output over a period and presumably for the future as well. If we assume that no idle capital should be allowed to exist and further that new capital may at times be forced to remain idle before demand picks up, the best way will be to drop the discrimination between old and new capital or between the initial and the terminal period, and to select our regions so as to minimise the average capital used over the years of the planning period, irrespective of the point at which investment is made. In most cases we have therefore considered the minimisation of capital in use over the entire period.

The capital minimizing model is now formulated as below:

Model 3

Minimise $\qquad\qquad \sum_p \sum_i {}_p b_{ip} x_i,$ $\qquad\qquad$ (4.13)

subject to

$$(1 - a_{ii})\, {}_p x_i + \sum_j a_{ij} \cdot {}_p x_j - \sum_q {}_{pq} x_i + \sum_q {}_{pq} x_i = {}_p f_i, \qquad (4.14)$$

$$ {}_p x_i \leqslant {}_p \bar{x}_i. \qquad\qquad (4.15)$$

However, in a situation where part of the total capital has already been put into definite forms and cannot be redirected usefully, the more relevant consideration is the best utilisation of incremental rather than total capital, and the formulation of the problem becomes a little more complicated. We have now to consider only incremental capital. But incremental capital may go into a new installation or into expansion of an already existing unit. Therefore this new capital in use is divided into two kinds: (*a*) that used for the substantial expansion of an existing unit; (*b*) that used in a completely new installation. The capital employed in the two situations will have different productivity. We now consider in the objective function only the incremental capital, rather than total capital, and in the constraint condition we consider satisfaction of only the incremental output required due to an increase in final demand.

Model 4

Minimise $\qquad \sum_p \sum_i {}_p b_i^s \cdot {}_p x_i^s + \sum_p \sum_i {}_p b_i^n \cdot {}_p x_i^n,$ $\qquad$ (4.16)

subject to

$$(1 - a_{ii})\, {}_p x_i^s - \sum_j a_{ij}\, {}_p x_j^s - \sum_p {}_{pq} x_i^s + \sum_q {}_{pq} x_i^s + (1 - a_{ii})\, {}_p x_i^n - \sum_j a_{ij} \cdot {}_p x_j^n$$

$$- \sum_q {}_{pq} x_i^n + \sum_q {}_{qp} x_i^n = \Delta_p f_i. \qquad (4.17)$$

MODELS MAXIMISING PROFIT

The third set of objective functions refer to the maximisation of profit. The rate of return on total capital is a natural extension of the objective function minimising capital in use. The profits per unit calculated here are not discounted for the future. The profit is considered at the point of time or over the interval for which balance relations have been used. This approach, therefore, does not bring in inter-temporal considerations. This limitation has to be accepted as the size of the programme becomes prohibitively large if this new complication is introduced.

In this group of models the balance relations of earlier models are retained but the objective function has been changed. The objective function now formulated is as follows:

Model 5

Maximise $$\sum_p \sum_i {}_p\pi_i \cdot {}_pb_i \cdot {}_px_i. \tag{4.18}$$

In this model we considered only the industries in the group, without going into the problem of cost of overhead facilities for the group as a whole. In new or underdeveloped regions large amounts of facilities have to be created, although in many regions they will not be adequately used in the short run. But these regions may have a higher productivity of capital and a more favourable situation regarding land, labour etc. A choice therefore has to be made, keeping both these factors in mind. An 'other' sector is introduced, which embraces all sectors except the industries introduced explicitly in the model. In a developed region this residual sector is being adequately utilized. In an under-developed region the residual sectors are poorly developed or non-existent. The overhead facilities that are immediately available in a developed region have to be created for the new industries in an under-developed region, possibly with a low intensity of use. But overhead facilities cannot be created below a certain scale. The industries considered in the model will therefore have to pay for the overhead facilities to be provided on this minimum scale, although they may not be used in full, at least in the beginning. With residual sector industries coming in later on, the situation will gradually improve in favour of the 'new' area, provided it has other favourable factors. Hence we now consider the 'overhead' as a sector embracing industries other than those considered explicitly in the model.

The cost of such underutilised overhead facilities is therefore brought into the model, which is described below:

Model 6

Maximise $$\sum_p \sum_i {}_p\pi_i \cdot {}_pb_i \cdot {}_px_i - \sum_p {}_p\pi_o \; {}_pb_o \cdot {}_ps_o, \tag{4.19}$$

subject to

$$(1-a_{ii}) \, {}_px_i - \sum_j {}_pa_{ij} \cdot {}_px_j - a_{io} \, {}_px_o - \sum_q {}_{pq}x_i + \sum_q {}_{qp}x_i = {}_pf_i, \tag{4.20}$$

$${}_px_o \geqslant \sum_i a_{oi} \, {}_px_i + a_{oo} \, {}_px_o + {}_pf_o, \tag{4.21a}$$

or $${}_px_o - {}_ps_o - \sum_i a_{oi} \cdot {}_px_i - a_{oo} \, {}_px_o = {}_pf_o, \tag{4.21b}$$

$${}_px_o \geqq {}_p\bar{x}_o \quad \text{(scale constraint)}, \tag{4.22a}$$

or $${}_px_o - {}_ps_o = {}_p\bar{x}_o, \tag{4.22b}$$

$${}_px_i \leqslant {}_p\bar{x}_i. \tag{4.23}$$

Equation (4.20) gives the requirement of the 'overhead sector' output to the group and to itself. Equation (4.21 a) gives the scale constraint for the overhead group, which ensures that a minimum of overhead output has to be produced. This conditon, may, however, create a surplus, as in equation (4.21 b). This idle overhead has to be paid for by the industries included in the group. Hence in the objective function (4.19) we have the 'profit' of all sectors less the penalty for the unused capacity in overhead. The penalty for 'idle' overhead defines the level at which overhead facilities remain unused in a less developed area. It is obvious that once development rises above a certain level, overhead investment or infrastructure is utilized above the penalty limit, the slack disappears and higher profits emerge, making the region viable in an economic sense.

5. THE APPLICATION OF LINEAR PROGRAMMING MODELS: 1

MODELS MINIMISING LABOUR AND TRANSPORT COST

In this chapter and those following, the models described in Chapter 4 are implemented empirically. Two groups of experiments are carried out. The first set is carried out on data relating to the Indian Union, on the basis of the input–output tables of 1954 (Dhar, 1965). The commodities chosen for this set of experiments are coal, cement, cotton, jute, iron and steel and sugar. The selection of the commodities was determined mainly with an eye to their importance as intermediate products produced in only a few regional centres in India. The model for this demonstration has been described in (4.6)–(4.9).

In the first experiment, the assumption is made that there is no capacity limit on production in any sector in any region. This implies that an optimal solution will have only to conform to the restrictions stated in (4.7)–(4.8). Table 5.1 gives the results of this experiment, along with the corresponding actual data. Some useful conclusions may be drawn. It can be seen that the deviation between optimal and actual is not very large so far as production is concerned. But considerable deviations exist between the actual and the optimal interregional flows. However, this should not be interpreted as a sign of the inefficiency of the trade pattern, for two reasons.

First, in such experiments the actual capacity levels are bound to affect interregional flows. The situation is, therefore, bound to change once realistic capacity limits are introduced. But this unrestricted flow and its direction still gives some useful information. In some regions the optimal level of production is higher than the actual output. Such cases show the comparative advantages of producing more in these regions in the existing cost and transport situation. In a later experiment this assumption of unlimited capacity is withdrawn, and capacity limits are imposed in some regions, so as to describe a more realistic situation.

The second reason for the large difference between the actual and the optimal is due to a more difficult technical hurdle. It may be seen that in our regional classification (see Table A5.2 in the appendix to this chapter, p. 72) each region is a reasonably large area, in which two or more states are combined together. In such cases, the distance between two points on either side of the border between two states, although it may be quite small, is still taken to be the average distance between the

[25]

TABLE 5.1. *Actual and optimal production and optimal interregional flow of commodities*† (*in crores*‡ *of Rs.*)

From Region/Sector			To Region/Sector				
			1	2	3	4	5§
1	Coal	i	19.7				
		ii	17.8	6.2	1.3	0.2	0.1
	Sugar	i	18.9				
		ii	23.1	5.0	0.2	0.0	0.0
	Cement	i	5.1				
		ii	17.1	0.1	0.0	0.0	0.0
	Cotton	i	121.9				
		ii	120.6	1.7	0.3	0.2	0.0
	Jute	i	108.8				
		ii	120.3	2.0	1.7	0.4	0.3
	Iron and steel	i	26.7				
		ii	32.6	5.1	3.7	2.1	0.9
2	Coal	i		17.8			
		ii	5.5	26.2	1.4	0.7	1.3
	Sugar	i		82.7			
		ii	1.1	92.8	11.4	0.0	4.9
	Cement	i		5.7			
		ii	3.3	6.5	0.0	0.0	0.0
	Cotton	i		257.8			
		ii	0.7	244.6	1.1	0.1	0.3
	Jute	i	6.6				
		ii	0.2	0.2	2.2	0.2	0.4
	Iron and steel	i		26.9			
		ii	6.8	47.1	3.7	1.3	0.8
3	Coal	i			11.2	0.7	
		ii	0.0	0.0	8.7	1.0	0.2
	Sugar	i			24.8		
		ii	0.0	0.2	19.7	0.1	1.0
	Cement	i			5.6		
		ii	0.0	2.3	8.7	0.2	1.8
	Cotton	i			155.4		
		ii	0.1	3.6	145.7	0.4	5.9
	Jute	i					
		ii	0.1	0.2	0.4	0.1	0.3
	Iron and steel	i	0.8	10.2	27.2	6.7	
		ii	0.0	0.4	2.9	0.2	0.3
4	Coal	i				4.8	
		ii	0.0	0.0	0.0	3.2	0.0
	Sugar	i				44.2	
		ii	0.1	0.0	0.4	47.9	1.0
	Cement	i				6.3	
		ii	0.2	0.2	0.1	6.7	0.1

TABLE 5.1 (*cont.*)

From Region/Sector		To Region/Sector 1	2	3	4	5
Cotton	i				*222.3*	
	ii	1.0	0.6	3.0	*221.7*	2.3
Jute	i					
	ii	0.06	0.08	0.32	1.4	0.09
Iron and steel	i	0.9	0.7			
	ii	0.0	0.0	0.1	*1.6*	0.2
5 Coal	i					*7.8*
	ii	0.0	0.0	0.0	0.0	*6.3*
Sugar	i			12.0	2.4	*47.6*
	ii	0·0	2.4	6.2	0.0	*34.7*
Cement	i					*5.1*
	ii	0.0	0.0	1.1	0.0	*5.1*
Cotton	i					*253.8*
	ii	0.6	8.8	15.2	6.6	*278.1*
Jute	i	2.8	4.7	4.5	1.5	*21.5*
	ii	0.0	0.0	0.8	0.2	*24.6*
Iron and steel	i					*11.9*
	ii	0.0	0.3	1.6	0.8	*2.8*

† Italicised figures in the diagonal cells, e.g. from region 1 to region 1, or from region 2 to region 2, represent production figures; while all other figures represent interregional trade flows i signifies optimal and ii actual.
‡ 1 crore = 10 million.
§ The numbered regions are defined in Table A 5.2, p. 72.

centres of the two regions in an economic sense. Naturally, therefore, some flows between two such neighbouring points in the two regions appear in the aggregated solution as inefficient cross-hauling, whereas in fact they are not. The programming model in such cases eliminates all such extensive border trade between the regions, because of our failure to give a proper definition of distance. The remedy for this is clearly to increase the number of regions to a more realistic level and to do the experiment on a more elaborate basis.

TABLE 5.2. *Production capacity limits (in crores of Rs.)*

Region 1		Region 2	
Commodity	Capacity	Commodity	Capacity
Coal ($_1x_1$)	17.8	Cotton ($_2x_4$)	244.6
Sugar ($_1x_2$)	18.9	Region 5	
Cement ($_1x_3$)	1.7		
Cotton ($_1x_4$)	120.6	Commodity	Capacity
		Sugar ($_5x_2$)	34.7

A number of limits to capacity are introduced as in Table 5.2, based on *a priori* knowledge of the various regions and their products. [Table 5.3 gives the results of the subsequent experiment]. For an area known to be a small producer it is assumed that it is already working to full capacity.

TABLE 5.3. *Optimal and actual production and flows* (*in crores of Rs.*)

From Region/Sector			To Region/Sector				
			1	2	3	4	5
1	Coal	i†	17.8				
		ii†	17.8	2.4			
	Sugar	i	18.9				
		ii	18.9	5.0			
	Cement	i	11.7				
		ii	1.7	0.1			
	Cotton	i	120.6				
		ii	120.6	1.6			
	Jute	i	118.4	0.5			
		ii	120.2	2.0			
	Iron and steel	i	27.8				
		ii	32.6	5.1			
2	Coal	i	1.4	19.7			
		ii	5.5	26.2			
	Sugar	i		81.0			
		ii	1.1	92.8			
	Cement	i	2.9	8.7			
		ii	3.3	6.5			
	Cotton	i		244.6			
		ii	0.7	244.6			
	Jute	i		3.3			
		ii	0.2	4.1			
	Iron and steel	i		28.3			
		ii	6.8	47.1			
3	Coal	i			11.2		
		ii			8.7		
	Sugar	i			27.0		
		ii			19.7		
	Cement	i	0.2		5.8		
		ii	0.0		8.7		
	Cotton	i		5.1	160.5		
		ii		3.6	145.7		
	Jute	i			4.6		
		ii			0.4		
	Iron and steel	i		9.7	25.9	5.9	
		ii			2.9	0.2	

TABLE 5.3 (*cont.*)

From Region/Sector			To Region/Sector				
			1	2	3	4	5
4 Coal	i					4.8	
	ii					3.2	
Sugar	i					46.6	
	ii					47.9	
Cement	i					6.3	
	ii					6.7	
Cotton	i		1.2	7.3		233.0	
	ii		0.9	0.6		221.7	
Jute	i					1.6	
	ii					1.4	
Iron and steel	i		0.8				
	ii		0.0				
5 Coal	i			0.1	0.3	0.0	8.3
	ii			0.0	0.0	0.0	6.3
Sugar	i			1.6			34.7
	ii						34.7
Cement	i			0.2	2.4		5.3
	ii			0.1	2.4		5.1
Cotton	i						53.8
	ii						278.0
Jute	i						2.5
	ii						2.5
Iron and steel	i						2.3
	ii						2.8

† i optimal;   ii actual.

It can be seen that the introduction of a number of capacity constraints improves the nature of the agreement between the actual and the optimal flow, without bringing about any major difference from the previous exercise. This fact demonstrates that the exercises have considerable validity even without any capacity restrictions and that the relative advantages of the different regions may be detected even without such capacity limits.

To what extent is the optimal conditioned by our knowledge and assumptions of the present? Any programming problem has to face the possibility that the system of constraints has a significant influence on the optimal solutions. The more they are made realistic the more does the optimal solution follow the actual solution. One has to steer a course between the present set-up with its rigidity and the future set-up with its vague flexibilities. In most cases we have tried to combine existing norms and constraints with possible changes, as envisaged by the Planning Commission and other bodies of informed opinion. The extent to which our formulations have left enough flexilibity in the system is hard to specify quantitatively. This problem is in fact, common to all planning and projection work.

6. THE APPLICATION OF LINEAR PROGRAMMING MODELS: 2

MODELS MINIMISING LABOUR AND TRANSPORT

In this section model 1 is used with a different group of industries, i.e. coal, iron and steel, engineering and transport. As explained earlier, three types of objective function are tried out on the models described in Chapter 4. In the first set the objective function seeks to minimise the cost of labour and transport per unit of output. While generally a labour minimum solution does not seem very relevant for India, the kind of skilled labour that goes into iron and steel, engineering, etc., is certainly a scarce commodity. The transport element in the objective function refers only to movements to meet final demand; the cost of intermediate transport from factory to factory is given in a separate transport sector in the empirical exercise for 1971 and 1975.

The choice of sectors in the second series of experiments is made keeping in mind the concept of an industrial complex in developing economies, particularly of the heavier type of industries. It is generally assumed that these industries are largely public sector enterprises, needing a high level of direct government investment. These industries therefore need a proper location criterion, as public investments do raise the question of removing regional disparities while stimulating growth in the country as a whole.

Table 6.1 gives the optimal production for 1961, 1971 and 1975 while Table 6.2 gives the relative ranking of the regions by optimal values of production for the regions The relative final demand and capacities are given in the appendix to this chapter, in Table A 6–9.10 and 9.12 along with other relevant information.

Table 6.2, showing the optimal and actual figures for 1961, shows that in coal, iron and steel and engineering, at least for the more efficient producers, actual ranking is not generally very different from optimal ranking. This is to be expected, since in a competitive set-up an approach to efficient production is the best guarantee of success. However, the interesting thing is that in 1971 and 1975 the relative positions of the regions are gradually shifting.

In coal region 1 is the biggest producer in the optimal solution for 1961, though second to region 2 in actual production. In 1971 and 1975, however, we find that region 2 has taken over and we may therefore say that the actual is possibly nearer to the true optimal situation: region 1

TABLE 6.1 *Models 1 and 2, optimising labour and transport cost (in crores of Rs.)*

Region	Actual 1961	Optimal		
		1961	1971	1975
		Coal		
1	36.96	39.28*	97.67	110.80
2	54.11	51.57	176.44*	411.59
3	13.42	14.52	62.12*	155.30*
5	2.02	2.16	12.40*	31.00*
6	7.54	8.01	15.92*	39.80*
		Iron and steel (1)		
1	64.35	0.0	2.14	0.0
2	82.14	151.76	426.24*	1332.00*
3	0.31	0.0	14.46	303.21
6	5.25	0.0	0.0	0.0
		Iron and steel (2)		
1	21.42	10.52*	462.22*	1073.75*
2	8.80	35.77	0.0	0.0
3	8.91	0.0	0.0	0.0
4	9.91	0.0	11.31	14.60
5	27.00	30.05	0.0	0.0
6	5.84	0.0	0.0	0.0
		Engineering (1)		
1	220.88	232.98	377.24	809.72
2	65.88	92.79*	0.0	0.0
3	33.74	0.0	0.0	0.0
4	44.98*	47.37	0.0	0.0
5	239.64*	337.55	722.38	1247.90
6	115.61*	0.0	55.94	0.0
		Engineering (2)		
1			184.25	407.25
2			0.0	0.0
3			34.39	57.94
4			263.15*	443.26
5			109.50*	184.45*
6			0.0	0.0
		Transport		
1			362.09	613.17
2			233.02	426.46
3			317.13	522.54
4			94.27	141.01
5			351.62	545.30
6			280.66	429.20

* Full capacity production.

TABLE 6.2. *Ranking by volume of production in models 1 and 2 optimising labour and transport cost*

Sector	Rank by actual production	Rank by optimal production		
		1961	1971	1975
Coal	2	1	2	2
	1	3	1	3
	3	5	3	1
	6	6	6	6
	5	2	5	5
Iron and steel (1)	2	2		
	1	1	2	2
	6	3	3	3
	3	4	1	
		5		
		6		
Iron and steel (2)	2	2		
	1	1	1	1
	5	3		
	3	4	2	2
	4	5		
	6	6		
Engineering (1)	1	1	5	5
	6	4	1	1
	5	5	6	
	2	6		
	4	2		
	3	3		
Engineering (2)			5	5
			1	1
			6	6
			4	4
Transport			1	1
			5	5
			3	3
			6	6
			2	2
			4	4

is not able to catch up and in 1975 falls into third place, giving up the second position to region 3.

In iron and steel (1) region 2 take sthe highest rank from 1961 through 1975, as well as in the actual production figure for 1961. Region 1 again drops from second position in 1961 to third position, giving region 3 the lead. Full capacity production is achieved only by region 2, showing its overall competitive strength.

In iron and steel (2) region (1) takes over the lead from region in 1971, and the other regions in fact drop out. Region 1 produces to full capacity. In engineering (1) and (2) region 1 gives way to region 5 in 1971 and 1975, showing the competitive strength of this region in relatively foot-loose industries. Region 5 produces to full capacity. Region 4 is also doing well, and achieves full capacity production.

As our capacity figures for 1971 and 1975 are rather arbitrary it is quite conceivable that regions producing to full capacity will improve their position if restraints on capacity are relaxed. Hence production to full capacity is a better sign of efficient production and relative competitive strength than actual ranking.

Several general comments can be made on these tables. The first is that the traditional superiority of region 1 in the earlier years seems to be increasingly challenged by up-and-coming regions. There is also a wider dispersal of industrial development. It can be seen that region 3, a backward region, is certainly edging its way up in iron and steel, while region 5 is doing the same in engineering. The attributed capacities are fully utilized in iron and steel in region 2 and in engineering in region 5. These regions thus show a positively bright picture for development. The position of region 1 is certainly not so promising, except possibly in engineering (1).

7. THE APPLICATION OF LINEAR
PROGRAMMING MODELS: 3

MODELS MINIMISING CAPITAL COST

In the second group of experiments we consider minimisation of capital in use as the objective in various alternative forms of the model. In under-developed countries capital is a bottleneck to expansion more often than labour, even of the skilled variety. Skilled labour can be trained up by a crash programme, but capital accumulation is more difficult and is a slower process. The question however remains how to formulate the minimum capital objective. We can take up the question of new capital or total capital; we can think of expansion of existing units and also of new installations. None of the approaches is completely satisfactory. The new capital approach would be useful if we were optimising for a short-run terminal point. If one covers a long period the new capital of the first few years may become old capital at a later stage. Further, in a country with a capital shortage, obsolete or old capital should have its own place and full capacity utilisation of all types of capital is de-sirable. All these considerations have been discussed in some detail in Chapter 4.

Table 7.1 gives the optimal production by regions in 1961, 1971 and 1975 for different types of capital as defined in the model. Table 7.2 gives rankings of the same for the different types of capital.

Coal production is seen to be stretched to its limit from 1971 to 1975. All the regions except region 1 are producing to the attributed full capa-city. Production is rising in regions 2–6, while some loss of production is evident in region 1. Region 1 thus shows poor prospects for coal in a period of rapid expansion. In the solution for substantial expansion, however, region 3 has the lead, indicating significant possibilities for expansion in this region. A comparison between the total capital minimising solution and the substantial expansion solution for 1961 shows that substantial expansion has a definite advantage.

Coming to iron and steel (1) and (2), we find that region 1 has an advantage over the others, particularly in iron and steel (2). But region 1 is not producing to full capacity. Region 2 definitely has a lead in 1971 and 1975 in iron and steel (1) and is producing to full capacity, while region 5 shows the same superiority in iron and steel (2). In the substan-tial expansion solution for 1961 we again find a different situation; region 1 has the highest efficiency for iron and steel (1).

2-2

TABLE 7.1. *Model 3, minimising capital use.* (*Optimal production in crores of Rs.*)

Region	Production by substantial expansion (model 4)	Total capital model 3		
		1961	1971	1975
		Coal		
1		39	95.71	88.54
2		102*	176.44*	441.10*
3	176	81*	62.12*	155.30*
5		8*	12.40*	31.00
6		8*	15.92*	39.80*
		Iron and steel (1)		
1	557			
2			330.42*	1315.24*
3			116.32	363.50
		Iron and steel (2)		
1			182.28	413.84
2		92		
3				
4		51*		
5		95	286.80*	670.28*
6				
		Engineering (1)		
1			634.63*	1096.32*
2				
3				
4				
5	435	520	479.84	920.15
6				
		Engineering (2)		
1	355	136*	173.18	397.11
2				
3				
4		14*	34.40*	57.94*
5		45	263.15*	443.26*
6			109.50*	184.45*
		Transport		
1	121	81	328.88	525.22
2	207	147	224.18	426.64
3	305	216	328.30	529.15
4	68	49	91.04	138.87
5	26	157	378.29	613.17
6	188	133	279.36	429.20

* Full capacity production.

TABLE 7.2. *Ranking of regions by volume of production in optimal solution by models 3 and 4*

Sector	Substantial expansion model 4 1961	Total capital use model 3		
		1961	1971	1975
Coal	3	2	1	2
		3	2	3
		5	3	1
			6	5
			5	6
Iron and steel (1)			2	2
			3	3
				1
Iron and steel (2)		1	5	5
		5	1	1
		4		
Engineering (1)	5	5	1	1
			5	5
Engineering (2)	1	5	5	5
		1	6	1
		6	1	6
			4	4
Transport	3	5	5	5
	2	3	3	3
	6	1	1	1
	1	6	6	6
	4	2	2	2
	5	4	4	4

In engineering (1), region 1 has the lead in 1971 and 1975 taking over from region 5 which had the lead in 1961. In region 1 full capacity production is being achieved. But the substantial expansion solution for 1961 gives the lead to region 5.

We have seen in Table 7.1 that capital minimising by the substantial expansion solution is different from the total capital minimising solution with overall capital–output ratios rather than marginal ratios.

Further it should be noted that no restriction has been placed on substantial expansion. However, if it is carried beyond a certain point the specific advantages it has compared with new installations may become ineffective, and it may become more expensive than new installations. The limits to substantial expansion are much harder to define and it is difficult to consider them in a linear framework. The question of substantial expansion as against new installation also involves the planning horizon and the scale of expansion which is being visualized. These considerations may substantially change the situation.

It may also be noted that if we consider substantial expansion as a possibility the result puts all production in the optimal solution into this category rather than new installations. This demonstrates how much more economical it is in the short run, from the point of view of capital, to expand an already established area rather than new areas. However, the substantial expansion model was not applied to the later periods, as the full utilisation of total capital was considered more important in the long run.

The significance of the total capital minimum solution is that efficiency ranking is not generally changed by the introduction of this new concept. It may be seen that regions 2 and 3 still lead in coal and iron and steel, while regions 1 and 5 lead in engineering. It can broadly be said that both the models given in Chapter 6 and the model proposed in the present chapter lead to similar results.

8. THE APPLICATION OF LINEAR
PROGRAMMING MODELS: 4

THE MODEL MAXIMISING PROFIT

In our earlier formulation of the objective function specific aspects of the cost component, e.g. labour or capital, were taken up, with the idea that these have a physical interpretation and in an economy with scarce capital or scare labour such specific and physically precise objectives may be of importance in the short run. But the theory of competitive capitalism holds that the price of each factor is the best indicator of its scarcity and under such conditions a profit-maximising solution should automatically price each factor according to its relative scarcity. Such a theory may be valid in the long run, provided the conditions of perfect competition are met. But how about the profit concept and its use in a short-run solution? In this chapter we take up the conventional objective function of profit maximisation. The model has been discussed in (4.18) and (4.19–4.23); the measurement technique for profit is discussed in the appendix to Chapters 6–9, pp. 75–98.

In deriving profit solutions we consider two alternative sets of constraints. In one set the question of overhead costs is not raised because in an under-developed region, although the current overhead cost may be high, with growing overhead facilities it may show a profit, as the overhead cost will be distributed over an expanding set of activities. Hence a penalty is charged if the residual sectors have a level of low production. This means that a region with high residual production derives the advantage of overhead without any extra charge. The model has been discussed in more detail in Chapter 4. Tables 8.1and 8.2 give the solutions for production and the ranks of the regions.

It will be seen that as far as coal is concerned every region is producing to capacity. Regions 2 and 1 take the leading positions in the relative ranking. These are established areas for coal production and a profit-maximising solution gives them the highest ranking. A comparison with the solution by minimising capital cost shows that in the short run the minimum capital solution favours region 3 over region 1 in 1975, although the profit-maximising solution does not. Again, region 1 does not produce to full capacity in the minimum capital solution, but does in the maximum profit solution.

Coming to iron and steel (1) and (2) we again find that regions 1 and 2 are more profitable, though not more capital-saving. Region 5 manages

Table 8.1. *Models 5 and 6 maximising profit (in crores of Rs.)*

		Optimal production		
		1971		1975
Region/Sector		With overhead constraint (model 6)	Without overhead constraint (model 5)	Without overhead constraint
Coal	1	133.12*	133.12*	332.80*
	2	176.44*	176.44*	441.10*
	3	62.12*	62.12*	155.30*
	5	12.40*	12.40*	31.00*
	6	15.92*	15.92*	39.80*
Iron and steel (1)	1	257.44*	257.44*	804.50
	2	426.24*	216.25	1332.00
	3	116.32*	—	299.23
Iron and steel (2)	1	459.45	2.33	491.38
	2	—	58.71	—
	3	37.60*	37.60*	—
	4	48.67*	48.62*	113.63*
	5	248.67*	286.80*	432.66
	6	45.34*	45.34*	105.95*
Engineering (1)	1	634.63	634.63	1096.32
	2	—	—	—
	3	164.38	164.38	283.97*
	4	—	—	—
	5	—	—	—
	6	473.44	272.48	560.68
Engineering (2)	1	302.01	230.48	740.39*
	2	—	—	37.10*
	3	—	—	57.48*
	4	—	—	57.94*
	5	263.15*	263.15*	443.26*
	6	109.50*	109.50*	184.45*
Transport	1	2716.09	335.24*	645.45*
	2	253.26	220.17*	429.05*
	3	667.80*	324.09*	530.03*
	4	367.90*	97.37*	125.53*
	5	1704.50*	367.16*	565.07*
	6	1082.50*	291.57*	455.96*

* Full capacity production.

to maintain its position in both the solutions, though not against region 1 in the profit solution. Region 1 is a full-capacity producer in the profit maximum solution, though not in the other solution.

In engineering (1) region 1 has a lead over the other regions in both the solutions, e.g. it is both most profitable and least capital-using, and region 5 loses its position in the profit solution to region 6 and region 3.

TABLE 8.2. *Ranking of the regions in the optimal solution for the profit-maximising models 5 and 6*

	Ranking of regions		
	1971		1975
Region/Sector	Without overhead constraint (model 5)	With overhead constraint (model 6)	Without overhead constraint (model 5)
Coal	2	2	2
	1	1	1
	3	3	3
	6	6	6
	5	5	5
Iron and steel (1)	1	2	2
	2	1	1
		3	3
Iron and steel (2)	5	1	1
	2	5	5
	4	4	4
	6	6	6
	3	3	
	1	2	
Engineering (1)	1	1	1
	6	6	6
	3	3	3
Engineering (2)	5	1	1
	1	5	5
	6	6	6
			4. 3
			2
Transport	5	1	5
	1	5	1
	3	6	3
	6	3	6
	2	2	2
	4	4	4

In engineering 2 the two solutions again diverge. Region 1 has the lead in profit earning and region 5 in capital saving.

This divergence is made clear if we compare the relative capital-output ratios and the profit rates by sectors given in Table A 6–9.11 in the appendix. It will be seen that there is a definite positive correlation between capital using and profit making. The highest rates of profit are associated with greater use of capital. This is in fact quite reasonable, as better equipped industries prove more profit-worthy than industries having a small amount of capital per unit of output. In the short run, therefore, capital in low-profit areas may remain idle while expansion is sought in the more profitable areas. In a country with an acute scarcity of capital this may not be the best short-run solution for rational planning.

We have noted earlier the use of the concepts of overhead costs and residual sectors. The results of the model using these concepts present some interesting features. A comparison of the 1971 and 1975 optimal solutions with the 1971 solution taking into account overhead costs brings out some interesting features of the problem. It may be seen that the ranking for 1971 including overheads anticipates 1975 ranking better, indicating that the model is a better predictor of the future. For iron and steel (2) it may be seen that the ranking for 1971 and 1975 including overheads is identical; the same may be said of engineering (2), though not of transport.

9. THE PATTERN OF INTERREGIONAL TRADE FLOWS

THE REGIONAL TRADING POSITION

One of the objectives of the present set of exercises is to study the nature of interregional flows along with the location of production centres. The models have been so designed as to automatically give a set of optimal commodity flows from the regions according to minimum costs, whether of labour or capital, or maximum profit. The solutions for optimal interregional flows are given in Table 9.1.

It will be seen that the nature of the exchange relationship has not substantially changed over the years in any of the solutions, though volumes have changed substantially as demand and supply have shifted. New supply centres have emerged in some cases. Thus in 1975 region 1 is a supplier to region 3 in engineering, which it was not in 1971 or 1961. Some supply has changed directions. Region 1 was supplying coal to region 5 in 1961 but is not doing so in 1975. Similar changes may be noted in other areas. Region 2 is a source of supply of iron and steel to region 4 in 1971 and 1975. Region 5 is a supplier of engineering goods to region 3 again in 1971 and 1975, but not in 1961.

Table 9.2 shows the relative trading positions of the states according to the different models. It can be seen again that the relative position has not changed in the first two solutions. Regions which were not exporters are still not exporters, but there are changes in the volume of interregional trade.

It may be broadly concluded that new regions which are producing are not doing so in order to export, but only to support themselves. The increasing volume of home demand has made it possible for them to produce successfully, but not necessarily to compete with other regions which were already exporting. This is of course natural. Traditional exporters have lost part of their market because of local production, but local producers do not have the comparative advantages which would enable them to change the direction of interregional trade. One or two regions have, however, broken out of this limitation. Region 4 has moved from being a net importer to being a net exporter of iron and steel (2). Some structural changes are also seen in the optimal solution for profit. Thus in coal, region 6 is a net exporter in the profit maximum solution, while in all other formulations of the objective function it is a net importer. Region 4 is a net exporter in the optimal profit solution in

TABLE 9.1. *Interregional flows in different sectors in model 1 minimising labour and transport costs (in crores of Rs. at '60–1 prices)*

Sector	Regions 1	2	3	4	5	6
			Iron and steel (1)			
61					22.636	
71				9.020	9.005	23.252
75				12.550		20.840
61						
71						
75						
			Iron and steel (2)			
61						
71		399.035				
75		908.560				
			Engineering (1)			
61		47.064				25.191
71		113.164		105.373		
75		203.320	125.960	178.810		
			Engineering (2)			
61						
71		57.890	15.673	22.220		
75		105.57	71.380	40.66		
			Coal			
61			3.306		16.038	2.394
71					46.557	
75					70.120	
			Iron and steel (1)			
61	34.084		18.442		54.067	6.194
71	233.721		23.567	37.394	56.577	44.649
75	652.97			132.46	161.380	242.28
			Iron and steel (2)			
61	17.095		8.261			0.466
71			68.219	38.629	130.980	113.691
75			158.390	97.680	290.750	248.750
			Engineering (1)			
61			62.308			
71						
75						
			Engineering (2)			
61						
71						
75						

TABLE 9.1 (*cont.*)

Sector	Regions					
	1	2	3	4	5	6
			Coal			
61				2.851		
71					8.850	
75					13.480	
			Iron and steel (1)			
61				12.341		
71						
75					104.700	
			Iron and steel (2)			
61				7.550		
71						
75						
			Engineering (1)			
61						82.731
71			174.563			
75			179.990			415.260
			Engineering (2)			
61						
71			77.918			23.208
76			96.350			48.600

engineering and iron and steel, but not in the other solution. It is not difficult to make correct assessment of this change in the structure of interregional trade with changes in the objective function. The profit rate for 1975 gives a different ranking because regional rates of profit per unit of capital do not reflect the same pattern as the capital output ratios, as has been noted earlier. It is thus seen that a capital minimum or labour minimum solution is not necessarily the best solution from the more traditional point of view of profit.

Table 9.3 gives the cases where the three sets of solutions are similar and the cases where they are different. It will be seen that by and large the models give the same solution, though in six cases out of thirty capital and profit optimal solutions are different, i.e. a net exporter by one solution is not a net exporter by the other solution.

TABLE 9.2. *Regions as net exporters (+) or importers in the optimal solution (in crores of Rs. at '60–1 prices)*

Region Sector	Model minimising labour and transport			Model minimising capital		Model maximising profit	
	1961	1971	1975	1971	1975	1971	1975
			Coal				
1	+23	+41	+33	+42	+18	+9	+13
2	+51	+47	+70	+63	+97	+76	+94
3	−24	+9	+13	−9	+3	+10	+11
4	−3	−9	−13	−8	−12	−8	−14
5	−39	−64	−84	−65	−85	−63	−50
6	−2	−23	−21	−23	−21	−24	+17
			Iron and steel (1)				
1	−34	−234	−653	−129	−392	+193	−330
2	+112	+396	+1189	+304	+1172	+157	+1176
3	+12	−24	+105,	+78	+165	−61	+88
4	−12	−37	−132	−26	−125	−45	−185
5	−54	−57	−266	−188	−579	−175	−440
6	−6	−45	−242	−40	−242	−69	−309
			Iron and steel (2)				
1	−17	+399	+909	+112	+241	−72	−393
2	+26	−399	−113	−48	−113	+11	−120
3	0	−68	−158	−68	−158	−41	−190
4	−8	−39	−98	−50	−112	†	+1
5	0	−131	−291	+165	+392	+182	+188
6	−1	−114	−249	−111	−249	−80	−67
			Engineering (1)				
1	+72	+218	+508	+455	+722	+453	+752
2	−38	−113	−203	−113	−204	−113	−204
3	−8	−175	−306	−175	−306	−41	−77
4	0	−105	−179	−105	−179	−105	−179
5	+83	+358	+595	+171	+342	−199	−368
6	−25	−184	−415	−233	−415	+6	+75
			Engineering (2)				
1		+96	+218	+77	+199	+127	+281
2		−58	−106	−58	−106	−58	−73
3		−94	−168	−94	−168	−111	−143
4		−22	−41	−22	−41	−56	−114
5		+101	+145	+115	+164	+143	+217
6		−23	+49	−18	−49	−44	+319

† Just balances.

TABLE 9.3. *Nature of optimal solutions by sectors in different models*

Models	1971		1975	
	Same	Different	Same	Different
Labour, capital, profit	24	6	24	6
Labour, capital	27	3	29	1
Labour, profit	25	5	24	6
Capital, profit	24	6	25	5

10. THE DUAL FORMULATION OF
THE MODELS

INTRODUCTION

It is well known that all problems in linear programming can also be stated in an alternative form known as the dual of the original (or primal) problem. Such dual formulation shows many features of the problem from a different angle. Thus a minimum cost formulation can be stated in the dual as a resource-value maximising problem, and a profit maximising problem can be restated as a resource-cost minimising problem. In the following sections we discuss the dual formulations of the models given in Chapter 4, with the corresponding interpretations. Before going into the dual of the problems of Chapter 1 it may be useful to give a a simple case illustrating the formulation of the original problem with its dual.

The simplest type of programming problem of the transportation type may be formulated as follows:

Minimise
$$\sum_i \sum_j c_{ij} x_{ij}, \tag{10.1}$$

subject to
$$\sum_j x_{ij} \leq k_i, \tag{10.2}$$

$$\sum_i x_{ij} \geq r_j, \tag{10.3}$$

$$x_{ij} \geq 0, \tag{10.4}$$

where x_{ij} denotes the flows from the ith region to the jth region, c_{ij} the associated transport costs (including or excluding production costs), and k_i and r_j represents the capacity and requirements respectively of the regions.

The 'implicit price' system follows from the dual formulation of the problem stated below:

Maximise
$$\sum_j v_j r_j - \sum_i u_i k_i, \tag{10.5}$$

subject to
$$v_j \leq u_i + c_{ij}, \tag{10.6}$$

$$v_j u_i \geq 0, \tag{10.7}$$

where v_j denotes the delivered value to the jth region, u_i is the rent charged at the ith location and c_{ij} is the cost of transportation.

The objective function thus maximises the net revenue earned, on

[48]

condition that no delivered value may exceed the imputed rent plus transport costs. The well known conditions of perfect competition are also satisfied by the optimal solution, i.e. the best firms will earn zero profit, so that

$$v_j - u_i = c_{ij}, \quad \text{if,} \quad x_{ij} > 0, \tag{10.8}$$

$$v_j - u_i < c_{ij} \quad \text{if,} \quad x_{ij} = 0. \tag{10.9}$$

The second condition of perfect competition is that regions or sectors where capacity is fully utilised have positive royalties and those having unutilised capacity earn zero royalties This is also satisfied and we have

$$u_i > 0, \quad \text{if,} \quad \sum_j x_{ij} = k_i, \tag{10.10}$$

$$u_i = 0, \quad \text{if,} \quad \sum_j x_{ij} < k_i. \tag{10.11}$$

This basic model of the dual programme with suitable modifications has been extended to a class of problems involving many sectors and many regions.

THE ASYMMETRIC DUAL

In the presentation given above we have given inequalities rather than equations. When equations are taken instead of inequalities some additional complications enter into the dual formulation. This is explained below:

Minimise
$$\sum_i \sum_j c_{ij} x_{ij}, \tag{10.12}$$

subject to
$$\sum_i x_{ij} = r_j, \tag{10.13}$$

$$\sum_j x_{ij} \leq k_i, \tag{10.14}$$

$$x_{ij} \geq 0. \tag{10.15}$$

If the problem is presented in this way the dual variables associated with equality become undetermined as to sign. This is explained below. The problem may also be presented as

Minimise
$$\sum_i \sum_j c_{ij} x_{ij}, \tag{10.16}$$

subject to
$$\sum_i x_{ij} \geq r_j, \tag{10.17}$$

$$\sum_i x_{ij} \leq r_j, \tag{10.18}$$

$$\sum_j x_{ij} \leq k_i, \tag{10.19}$$

$$x_{ij} \geq 0. \tag{10.20}$$

This is equivalent to the following problem.

Minimise $$\sum_i \sum_j c_{ij} x_{ij}, \tag{10.21}$$

subject to $$\sum_i x_{ij} \geq r_j, \tag{10.22}$$

$$-\sum_i x_{ij} \geq -r_j, \tag{10.23}$$

$$-\sum_j x_{ij} \geq -k_i, \tag{10.24}$$

$$x_{ij} \geq 0. \tag{10.25}$$

The dual of the above will be

Maximise $$\sum_j r_j(u_j - v_j) - \sum_i k_i w_i, \tag{10.26}$$

subject to $$u_i - v_i - w_j \leqslant c_{ji}, \tag{10.27}$$

or maximise $$\sum_j r_j u'_j - \sum_i k_i w_i, \tag{10.28}$$

subject to $$u'_i - w_j \leq c_{ij}, \quad u_i \geq 0, \tag{10.29}$$

$$v_i \geq 0, \tag{10.30}$$

$$u_i, v_i, w_i \geq 0, \quad w_i \geq 0, \tag{10.31}$$

$u'_i = u_i - v_i$ has undetermined sign.

It is thus obvious that the associated shadow variable corresponding to each requirement is $u_j - v_j$. Since $u_j - v_j$ can have any sign, the optimal solutions may be positive in some cases but negative in others. The obvious interpretation is that $u_j - v_j$ is the shadow price (loss) associated with the optimal solution while the w_is are the shadow rents. In the asymmetric dual, we state the problem without the pair of inequalities but simply leaving u, v, to be determined without restrictions as to the sign.

THE DUAL FORMULATION OF THE PRESENT PROBLEM

The problems we have are somewhat more elaborate, as the balance relations involve coefficients of the input–output model. Otherwise, they are analogous with the above.

Since the primal problem gives the f_is as final outputs and the k_is as capacities, it is obvious that the dual variables represent the shadow price of labour and transport of each sector and the associated rents, so that in the case of models 1 and 2 the dual model seeks to maximise the shadow revenue (labour units) of final output less the inputed rent subject to the restriction that the imputed cost of production cannot exceed the labour charge per unit. The dual relating models 3 and 4 relates to the shadow value of capital per unit of output, with the restriction that the shadow capital cost of each output must be less than the actual capital per unit of output in the market. The two models thus seek to fulfil the requirements by making the best use of the labour or capital available in the economy.

We shall now present the duals of the models described in Chapter 4. The models, as we have seen, are all based on a more or less similar balance relation and input–output technology, with several different types of preference functions.

Dual of model 1

Maximise
$$\sum_p \sum_i {}_pf_i \cdot {}_pw_i + \sum_p \sum_i px_i \cdot {}_p\delta_i + \sum_p \sum_q {}_{pq}T \cdot \mu, \tag{10.32}$$

subject to
$$\left(1 - \sum_i a_{ji}\right) \cdot {}_pw_j + {}_p\delta_j \leqq {}_pl_i, \tag{10.33}$$

$$_qw_i - {}_pw_i + {}_{pq}d \cdot {}_p\theta_i \cdot \mu \leqq {}_{pq}\tau_i, \tag{10.34}$$

$$_pw_i - {}_qw_i + {}_{qp}d \cdot {}_q\theta_i \cdot \mu \leqq {}_{pq}\tau_i,$$

$$\mu, {}_p\delta_i \leqq 0, \tag{10.35}$$

$_pw_i$ have unrestricted sign.

Dual of model 2

Maximise
$$\sum_p \sum_i {}_pf_i \cdot {}_pw_i + \sum_p \sum_i {}_px_i \cdot {}_p\delta_i, \tag{10.36}$$

subject to
$$\left(1 - \sum_j a_{ji}\right) \cdot {}_pw_i + {}_p\delta_i \leqq {}_pl_i, \tag{10.37}$$

$$_p\delta_i \leqq 0, \tag{10.38}$$

$_pw_i$ have unrestricted sign.

Dual of model 3

Maximise
$$\sum_p \sum_i {}_nf_i \cdot {}_pw_i + \sum_p \sum_i {}_p\bar{x}_i \cdot {}_p\delta_i, \tag{10.39}$$

subject to
$$\left(1 - \sum_i a_{ij}\right) \cdot {}_pw_j + {}_p\delta_j \leqq {}_pb_j, \tag{10.40}$$

$$_qw_i - {}_pw_i \leqq 0, \tag{10.41}$$

$$_pw_i - {}_qw_i \leqq 0, \tag{10.42}$$

$$_p\delta_i \leqq 0, \tag{10.43}$$

$_pw_i$ have unrestricted sign.

Dual of model 5

Minimise
$$\sum_p \sum_i {}_pw_i \cdot {}_rf_i + \sum_p \sum_i {}_p\bar{x}_i \cdot {}_p\delta_i, \tag{10.44}$$

subject to
$$(1 - \sum_j a_{ji}) \cdot {}_p w_i + {}_p \delta_i \geq {}_p \pi_i \cdot {}_p b_i, \qquad (10.45)$$

$$_q w_i - {}_p w_i \geq 0, \qquad (10.46)$$

$$_p w_i - {}_q w_i \geq 0, \qquad (10.47)$$

$$_p \delta_i \geq 0. \qquad (10.48)$$

$_p w_i$ undetermined in sign.

Dual of model 6

Minimise

$$\sum_p \sum_i {}_p w_i \cdot {}_p f_i + \sum_p {}_p f_o \cdot {}_p w_0 + \sum_p {}_p \delta_o \cdot {}_p \bar{x}_o + \sum_p \sum_i {}_p \delta_i \cdot {}_p \bar{x}_i, \qquad (10.49)$$

subject to

$$(1 - \sum_j a_{ji}) \cdot {}_p w_i - a_{oi} \cdot {}_p w_o + {}_p \delta_i \geq {}_p \pi_i \cdot {}_p b_i, \qquad (10.50)$$

$$-\sum_j a_{jo} \cdot {}_p w_j + (1 - a_{oo}) \cdot {}_p w_o + {}_p \delta_o \geq {}_p \pi_o \cdot {}_p b_0, \qquad (10.51)$$

$$_p w_o + {}_p \delta_o \geq {}_p b_0, \qquad (10.52)$$

$$_q w_i - {}_p w_i \geq 0, \qquad (10.53)$$

$$_p w_i - {}_q w_i \geq 0. \qquad (10.54)$$

$_p w_i \cdot {}_p w_0, {}_q w_i$, are undetermined in sign.

$$_p \delta_i \geq 0, \quad {}_p \delta_o \leq 0. \qquad (10.55)$$

The dual of model 1 seeks to attach implicit values in terms of labour units to the outputs and capacities for each sector, such that the revenue earned in meeting final demand, less the rent charge on capacity is maximised. The implicit values of outputs are undetermined as to sign, while the rent charges of capital are negative.

Tables 10.1–10.3 give the sets of implicit values for 1960–1, 1970–1 and 1974–5. The rents, as may be seen, are a charge on the revenue. Iron and steel (1) and (2) have no rent charges in 1960–1 and 1970–1, indicating the existence of extra capacity. In 1975 there is some change in regions 1 and 2. Coal has a rent change in 1961 and 1971, as also in 1975 for most regions, reflecting the comparatively fuller utilisation of capacity in many regions. Engineering has a rent charge in 1961 but less in 1970 and 1975.

In the case of coal the implicit price is quite high in regions 5, 6 and 4. A comparison shows that the trend of implicit price does not change in the future, at least up to 1975. We have made some changes in the co-efficient structure during 1970–5, but the relative positions of shadow prices and rent do not seem to be very different as far as the various sectors are concerned.

TABLE 10.1. *Dual values for model 1, year 1960–1*

Region	Coal Price	Coal Rent	Iron and steel (1) Price	Iron and steel (1) Rent
1	0.7786	− 0.2936	0.2564	
2	0.4697		0.2540	− 0.0194
3	1.6731	− 1.1207	0.3042	
4	3.0207	—	0.3677	—
5	3.7976	− 3.0477	0.3928	—
6	2.4937	− 1.7818	0.3384	

Region	Iron and steel (2) Price	Iron and steel (2) Rent	Engineering Price	Engineering Rent
1	0.3217	0	0.4600	− 0.2009
2	0.3048	− 0.0008	0.4612	− 0.3420
3	0.3550	0	0.4647	0
4	0.4185	0	0.4625	− 0.1831
5	0.4404	0	0.4567	− 0.2129
6	0.3894	0	0.4550	− 0.1705

TABLE 10.2. *Dual values for model 1, year 1970–1*

Region	Coal Price	Coal Rent	Iron and steel (1) Price	Iron and steel (1) Rent	Iron and steel (2) Price	Iron and steel (2) Rent
1	1.1006		0.7993		0.6777	
2	0.9704		0.7734		0.7112	
3	1.9201	0.6425	0.9049		0.7653	
4	2.6585		0.9546		0.7858	
5	2.7741	− 1.3086	0.9452		0.7845	
6	2.8898	1.3943	0.9784		0.7956	

Region	Engineering (1) Price	Engineering (1) Rent	Engineering (2) Price	Engineering (2) Rent	Transport Price	Transport Rent
1	0.6312		0.1875		0.4973	
2	0.6437		0.1750		0.4299	
3	0.7067		0.1410		0.4298	
4	0.7187		0.0875		0.4404	
5	0.6647	0.0360	0.1750		0.3889	
6	0.7202		0.2245		0.4579	

TABLE 10.3. *Dual values of model 1, year 1974–5*

Region	Coal		Iron and steel (1)		Iron and steel (2)	
	Price	Rent	Price	Rent	Price	Rent
1	1.1017		0.8709		0.7327	−0.0262
2	0.9715		0.8451	−0.0714	0.7662	
3	1.9212	−0.6425	0.9452		0.8230	
4	2.6596	—	1.0262		0.8408	
5	2.7752	−1.3086	1.0168		0.8395	
6	2.8909	−1.3943	1.0500		0.8506	

Region	Engineering (1)		Engineering (2)		Transport	
	Price	Rent	Price	Rent	Price	Rent
1	0.6576		0.7585		0.4974	
2	0.6701		0.7710		0.4299	
3	0.7331		0.8340	−0.1653	0.4404	
4	0.7451		0.8460	−0.1209	0.3890	
5	0.6911	−0.0168	0.7920	−0.1329	0.4579	
6	0.7466	—	0.8475	−0.1329	0.4579	

A comparative study of the shadow values over 1960–1, 1970–1 and 1975–6 does not show any perceptible difference, in spite of big changes in the demand structure and some changes in the coefficient structure. This constancy suggests that the relative advantages of the currently producing sectors will not be substantially altered.

MINIMISING CAPITAL COST

It should be noted that in this exercise transport was used partly as an exogenous sector, transport costs being assigned for the flows externally. This led to the imputed transport differentials being incorporated into the output prices. It will be shown now that when transport is completely isolated as an endogeneous sector the solution becomes rather different.

As soon as the problem is formulated with transport as a sector the structure of the dual system becomes very simple It may be seen that if the associated direct and indirect transport inputs are put into a distinct sector, the implicit prices (here a ratio) for all sectors other than transport become the same for all regions. There is one implicit price for each sector, whatever the region it originates from. The optimal solution fixes a unique shadow value for the outputs of the sectors other than transport. It is only when considering implicit transport prices that interregional differences reappear.

If we separate out transport as a sector and if there is free movement from region to region, then the production problem is decomposed into two problems. The first is to decide the unique shadow price for each sectoral output, irrespective of the regions, and the second is to attach a shadow price to each region's production of transport which cannot be imported or exported. In effect the programme thus tells us that if transport were free one could produce it in the least capital using region and take it anywhere. In order to arrive at the final solution, of course, one has to reintroduce the transport charges.

TABLE 10.4. *Dual values of model 3 minimising capital use, 1960–1*

Region	Coal		Iron and steel (1)		Iron and steel (2)	
	Price of final demand	Cost of capacity	Price of final demand	Cost of capacity	Price of final demand	Cost of capacity
1						
2		0.4254				
3	2.0047		6.8635	− 0.3799	4.8389	
4						
5		− 0.0454				− 0.3916
6						

Region	Engineering (1)		Engineering (2)		Transport	
	Price of final demand	Cost of capacity	Price of final demand	Cost of capacity	Price of final demand	Cost of capacity
1		− 0.2166			11.9467	11.90
2					9.5486	9.46
3	1.5362				8.1758	8.09
4					8.2270	8.16
5		− 0.2497			6.6137	6.56
6		− 0.1205			7.3067	7.25

The dual of model 3 seeks to attach implicit values to outputs and capacity in units of capital, so as to maximise the shadow worth in terms of capital of the final demand, less the charge on capital. However, the implicit valuation must be such that capital cost of the inputs and capacity per unit of output are less than or equal to the capital-output ratio. An important feature, as already mentioned in the system of equations, is that all regional implicit prices for any specific sector are identical, due

TABLE 10.5. *Dual values of model 3: 1970–1 and 1975–6*

Region	Coal		Iron and steel (1)		Iron and steel (2)	
	Price of final demand	Cost of capacity	Price of final demand	Cost of capacity	Price of final demand	Cost of capacity
1						
2		− 0.6348				
3		− 0.2087		− 0.3811		
4	2.2708	—	6.8304		4.8262	
5		− 0.2545				− 0.3941
6		− 0.1323				

Region	Engineering (1)		Engineering (2)		Transport	
	Price of final demand	Cost of capacity	Price of final demand	Cost of capacity	Price of final demand	Cost of capacity
1		− 0.0395			11.9529	
2					9.5604	
3	1.4102		2.4179		8.1871	
4				− 0.5262	8.2358	
5				− 0.0256	6.6209	
6				− 0.1354	7.3143	

NOTE. The dual solutions are identical for 1971–2 and 1975–6.
— Indicates capacity not provided for.

to the free flow of interregional trade without any transport charges, transport being an independent sector.

The high imputed price of iron and steel and engineering relatively to coal shows the comparatively lower use of capital per unit of output in these industries, i.e. increasing the output of steel requires less capital per unit than increasing the output of engineering or coal in the capital solution. The shadow price of transport again shows the relatively higher capital use in region 5, for example compared to region 1, suggesting that a cheaper capital solution will be available from region 1 than from region 5.

A very large number of regions show a zero rent charge, denoting the existence of surplus capacity. As was seen before, this occurs in most sectors except coal. It may also be seen that in most sectors regions with established industries have excess capacity, rather than new regions.

Models 4 and 5 are profit maximising models. Their duals are thus minimising models. The dual of model 4 seeks to attach shadow costs to outputs and capacities so that the cost of the required final demand together with the rent charge is minimised. The shadow values, however, must not be less than the profit on capital employed per unit. The inclusion of transport once again makes the set of shadow values unique except for transport. The rent charges are of course different. The signs of the shadow values are again undetermined.

It will be seen that the implicit cost of inputs of coal is negative in 1970–1 and 1975–6. Other costs are positive. This indicates a kind o subsidy to coal production. The rent charges are zero in many sectors in different regions, again showing the existence of excess capacity. In coal, however, there is a positive rent charge. Coal is thus an industry which is relatively inefficient but is producing at full capacity. Other industries are more efficient relative to coal, but have surplus capacity.

TABLE 10.6. *Dual values of model 5, year 1970–1*

Region	Coal		Iron and steel (1)		Iron and steel (2)	
	Cost of final output	Capital cost	Cost of final output	Capital cost	Cost of final output	Capital cost
1		1.2295		0.2616		
2		1.1295				
3	−1.2729	1.1429	0.1055		0.2199	0.0060
4		—				
5		1.1502				0.2996
6		1.2184				0.0432

Region	Engineering (1)		Engineering (2)		Transport	
	Cost of final output	Capital cost	Cost of final output	Capital cost	Cost of final output	Capital cost
1		0.0483			0.6569	
2						
3	0.3716	0.2734	0.2890		0.4123	
4					0.4283	
5				0.0615	0.3444	
6				0.1405	0.3823	

TABLE 10.7. *Dual values of model 5, year 1975–6*

Region	Coal — Cost of final output	Coal — Capital cost	Iron and steel (1) — Cost of final output	Iron and steel (1) — Capital cost	Iron and Steel (2) — Cost of final output	Iron and Steel (2) — Capital cost
1		0.5854		0.2554		
2		1.4847		0.0313		
3	−1.7137	1.5032	−0.0012		0.1757	
4		—				0.2829
5		1.5049				
6		1.5731				

Region	Engineering (1) — Cost of final output	Engineering (1) — Capital cost	Engineering (2) — Cost of final output	Engineering (2) — Capital cost	Transport — Cost of final output	Transport — Capital cost
1		0.0684		0.2311		0.6467
2		—		0.1988		0.4701
3	+0.3329	0.2653	—	0.0895		0.3935
4		—		0.0094		0.4136
5		—		0.3170		0.3326
6		—		0.4013		0·3698

PROFIT MAXIMISATION WITH CONSIDERATION OF
OVERHEAD COSTS

Model 5 is similar to model 4 in its basic structure except for two important points. An 'others' sector has been introduced, which is bigger than all the other sectors as it includes all the residual sectors. Further there is a 'floor' level of production for the 'others' sector, with a charge on unused capacity in others. This is a model which attempts to establish a measure for the cost of developing industries in an under-developed 'new' region.

Table 10.8 gives the dual solution for model 5. The shadow prices show many interesting features. The implicit costs of the inputs of all sectors are negative. Rent charges are positive in most places in 1970–1, showing full utilization of capacity in a number of regions. The implicit cost of inputs of overhead sector is however, low, in the comparatively less developed regions.

The basic structural difference between models 4 and 5 consists in the fact that model 5 has a technological constraint of a lower bound on overheads, with a penalty for unused surplus. An analysis of the solution in

Table 10.8. *Dual values of overhead model 6; 1970–1*

	Coal		Iron and steel (1)		Iron and steel (2)	
Region	Cost of final output	Capital cost	Cost of final output	Capital cost	Cost of final output	Capital cost
1		0.1854		5.1158		0.3059
2		0.0784		4.7651		
3		0.0758	−4.4584	4.7439	−1.9714	0.0590
4		—				
5		0.0758				
6		0.1432				0.0852

	Engineering (1)		Engineering (2)	
Region	Cost of final demand	Capital cost	Cost of final demand	Capital cost
1		0.1996		
2				
3	−0.0090	0.2157	−0.6701	
4				
5				0.3389
6				0.4456

	Overhead sector	
Region	Cost of final demand	Capital cost
1	−0.476	—
2	−0.335	—
3	−0.324	+0.067
4	−0.326	+0.066
5	−0.262	+0.095
6	−0.290	+0.082

the tables shows that this leads in many sectors to increased production in excess of final demand. This situation results in negative shadow prices in the different sectors with positive rent charges on capital installation. The economic interpretation of such a situation is that a form of production subsidies and rents has to be introduced to reach the optimal target subject to the technological constraints, and further that technological constraints force many regions to produce in excess of final demand.

11. SUGGESTIONS FOR FUTURE RESEARCH

The experiments carried out so far have been on models where variables were continuous. The question of time, if it entered at all, did so in a very simple and explicit manner. Further all non-linearities were scrupulously avoided, so as to make full use of the standard simplex procedures. It is, however, obvious that many of the very important complications of the problem are assumed away by our treatment. Work is now going on in the Applied Economics Unit, Jadavpur University, to extend the present analysis to take in these complications. Some of these problems have in fact been formulated in suitable theoretical models for future experimentation. In this chapter we shall take up the theoretical formulation of a few of these extended models as guidelines towards future experimentation. These new formulations involve the following techniques:

(1) The integer programming technique applied to locational problems;

(2) a quadratic formulation of the location problem;

(3) the use of variational techniques to solve locational problems involving time;

(4) time-optimal problems in location studies and the application of Pontryagin's Maximum Principles.

THE INTEGER PROGRAMMING APPROACH

It often happens that factories can operate only at a certain level of production in integral bounds. Similarly, capacity can often be created only by discrete jumps, because of the indivisibility or the lumpiness of the capital goods in question. In these cases any realistic solution is based on the assumption that if a factory has to be built in a region it must have one of a finite set of capacity bundles k^r. That is, building any factory with capacity less than an integral bound of k^r will cost the same as k^r. The formulation of one such problem may be considered.

Assume that each regional output can occur at specific levels k^r $(r = 1, 2, 3, ..., n)$ and $k^1, k^2 ... k^r$ are integral bounds. Then the model in our case may be reformulated as below.

Model 11.1

Minimise $\quad \sum_r \sum_p \sum_i {}_p l_i^r \cdot {}_p k_i^r \cdot {}_p x_i^r + \sum_p \sum_q \sum_i {}_{pq} x_i \cdot {}_{pq} \pi_i,$ \hfill (11.1) subject to

$$\sum_r (1 - a_{ii})\, _px_i \cdot {_pk_i^r} - \sum_r \sum_j {_pa_{ij}} \cdot {_px_j^r} \cdot {_pk_j^r} + \sum_p \sum_q {_{qp}x_i} - \sum_q {_{pq}x_i} \geq {_pf_i}, \quad (11.2)$$

$$\sum_p \sum_q \sum_i {_{pq}x_i} \cdot {_pd_q} \cdot {_pw_i} \leq \overline{T}, \quad (11.3)$$

$$\sum_r {_pk_i^r} \cdot {_px_i^r} = {_p\bar{k}_i}, \quad (11.4)$$

$$0 \leqslant {_px_i^r} \leq 1, \quad (11.5)$$

$${_px_i^r}\ \text{are integers.}$$

Solutions to problems formulated with an integer constraint of this type can be obtained by the cutting plane technique of Gomory (1963) or the 'branch and bound' method introduced by Doig & Land (1960). But for extended problems the computational burden of such procedures is often prohibitively large.

An alternative approach for simpler cases may be made by dynamic programming (Bellman & Dreyfus, 1962) methods. Take, for example, the following problem.

Let n_i denote the number of projects of type i and b_i the capital cost per unit; r_i the net return per unit of that type with the condition that no fractional projects are permitted. Let k be the available resources. Then the object is

$$\text{to maximise}\quad \Sigma r_i x_i, \quad (11.6)$$

$$\text{subject to}\quad \Sigma b_i n_i = k, \quad (11.7)$$

where n_i is integral and non-negative.

The limit on total funds available makes it necessary that the restraint $\Sigma b_i n_i \leq k$ say, with $b_i \geq 0$. We want to maximise the function R $(b_1, b_2, ..., b_n)$, when n is a non-negative integer.

Writing

$$R(b_1, b_2 \ldots b_N) = g_1(b_1) + g_2(b_2) + \ldots g_N(b_N), \quad (11.8)$$

we seek to embed the problem in a family of allocation processes. We consider the whole family of N projects with the restriction that allocation is to be made one at a time. An arbitrary amount is assigned to the last activity first – that is, the dynamic process is posed in reverse, starting with $N, N-1, ..., 1$.

Consider the sequence of functions

$$f_N(p), \quad (N = 1, 2, ..., x \geq 0), \quad (11.9)$$

$$f_N(b) = \max R(b_1, ..., b_N), \quad (11.10)$$

$$b_i \geq 0, \quad \Sigma b_i \leq k, \quad (11.11)$$

where $f_N(b)$ defines the best return from allocating b amounts to n activities. Whatever choice is made for b_N, we can consider the remaining resources as $f_{N-1}(k - b_N)$ and define total return as $g_N(b_N) + f_{N-1}(k - b_N)$, obtaining

$$f_N(b) = \max g_N(b_N) + f_{N-1}(k - b_N) \quad (N = 2, 3, ..., x = 0), \quad (11.12)$$

$$f_i(b) = g_1(b).$$

This is the well known principle of optimality. The principle states that given any decision, whatever it is, later decisions should be optimal for the states resulting from the first decision. The process thus consists of picking up the set of optimal policies of the $(n-1)$th state corresponding to the set of decisions regarding the nth stage and choosing the maximum combined result by enumerating all such combinations. This process is continued over all the N choices. Obviously if the dimensions of the problem are reduced integral restrictions may be tackled by dynamic programming techniques.

NON-LINEAR PROGRAMMING

Many of the problems we have been posing simply cry out for the application of non-linear techniques. Thus the objective functions involving profit or cost are most often non-linear and as output increases or decreases such functions change direction continuously. But in most of the problems we have examined such non-linear functions have not been admitted.

Assume, for example, that the capital-output ratio or the labour-output ratio rises with increasing output. Then a capital minimising problem may be formulated as below:

Minimise
$$\sum_p \sum_i {}_p\pi_i \cdot ({}_p\lambda_i \cdot {}_px_i), \quad (11.13)$$

subject to
$${}_p\lambda_j = {}_p\alpha_j + {}_p\beta_j \cdot {}_px_j, \quad (11.14)$$

or, by substitution, we get the expression

Minimise
$$\sum_p \sum_i \sum_j {}_p\pi_i \left({}_p\alpha_i + {}_p\beta_i + {}_px_j\right) {}_px_j, \quad (11.15)$$

subject to the balance restrictions stated in the models in Chapter 4.

Similarly, if we consider that profit may increase at first but subsequently fall with increases in output, we may restate the problem of profit maximisation as

Maximise
$$\sum_p \sum_i {}_p\pi_i \cdot {}_p\lambda_i \cdot {}_px_i, \quad (11.16)$$

where
$${}_p\lambda_i = p\alpha_i - {}_p\beta_i \cdot {}_px_i, \quad (11.17)$$

getting the quadratic expression

Maximise
$$\sum_p \sum_i \sum_j {}_p\pi_i({}_p\alpha_i \cdot {}_px_j - {}_p\beta_i \cdot {}_px_i \cdot {}_px_i), \quad (11.18)$$

subject to the restrictions as stated before.

Most of the problems we have put in a linear form may be more realistically formulated in non-linear form. Solutions of such problems are possible provided they satisfy some convexity properties and are well behaved, so that they satisfy the well known Kuhn–Tucker conditions. Experiments with such formulations are now being made in an attempt to find a more realistic approach to the problems.

THE VARIATIONAL APPROACH

An important class of location problems involves time in some form or other, as these problems are usually concerned with growth over time. The optimisation problem again and again comes up against the period over which the optimisation is to be carried out. Clearly it is numerically possible in some cases to treat it as several discrete points of time and do straightforward summation. But a more elegant and generalised solution can sometimes be obtained if we can formulate our problems in variational terms. Consider the following problem.

Minimise

$$\int \sum_p \sum_q \sum_i {}_{pq}T_i \cdot {}_{pq}x_i(t) \cdot dt, \tag{11.19}$$

subject to

$${}_px_i = \sum_j {}_pa_{ij} \cdot {}_px_j + {}_pC_i + {}_p\dot{S}_i + \sum_q {}_{pq}x_i - \sum_q {}_{qp}x_i, \tag{11.20}$$

$${}_pS_i = {}_pb_i \cdot {}_px_i, \tag{11.21}$$

$${}_pC_i \geqq 0, \quad \text{i.e.} \quad {}_pC_i - t_{ci}^2 = 0, \tag{11.22}$$

$${}_{pq}x_i - {}_{qp}x_i \geqq 0, \quad \text{i.e.} \quad {}_{pq}x_i - {}_{qp}x_i - {}_{pq}t_i^2 = 0, \tag{11.23}$$

$${}_px_i \geqq 0, \quad \text{i.e.} \quad {}_px_i - {}_pt_i^2 = 0. \tag{11.24}$$

Here the optimisation may be over a specific period of time taken.

We have the Euler expression F as

$$F = \sum_p \sum_q \sum_i {}_{pq}T_i \cdot {}_{pq}x_i + \sum_p \sum_i {}_p\lambda_i \big({}_px_i - \sum_j {}_pa_{ij} \cdot {}_px_j - {}_pC_i - {}_pb_i \cdot {}_p\dot{x}_i$$

$$- \sum_q {}_{pq}x_i + \sum_q {}_{qp}x_i \big) + \sum_p \sum_i {}_{pq}\eta_i \big({}_{pq}x_i - {}_{qp}x_i - {}_{pq}t_i \big)$$

$$+ \sum_i {}_p\theta_i \big({}_px_i - {}_pt_i^2 \big) + \sum_i {}_p\rho_i \big({}_pC_i - {}_pt_{ci}^2 \big), \tag{11.25}$$

where $\lambda, \mu, \eta, \theta, \rho$ are Lagrange multipliers.

Setting

$$\frac{\partial F}{\partial {}_px_i} - \frac{d}{dt} \cdot \frac{\partial F}{\partial {}_p\dot{x}_i} = 0, \quad \frac{\partial F}{\partial t_{ci}} = 0, \quad \frac{\partial F}{\partial {}_{pq}x_i} = 0, \quad \frac{\partial F}{\partial {}_{pq}t_i} = 0, \quad \frac{\partial F}{\partial {}_pt_i} = 0, \tag{11.26}$$

we get, therefore,

$${}_p\lambda_i - \sum_j {}_p\lambda_j \, {}_pa_{ij} - {}_pb_i \cdot {}_p\dot{\lambda}_i - {}_p\theta_i = 0, \tag{11.27}$$

$${}_{pq}T_i + {}_p\lambda_i + {}_{pq}\eta_i = 0. \tag{11.28}$$

This thus relates the Lagrange multipliers to the flow variables $_{pq}x_i$. We also get

$$_{pq}\eta_i \cdot {}_{pq}t_i = 0, \tag{11.29}$$

$$_p\theta_i \cdot {}_pt_i = 0, \tag{11.30}$$

$$_p\rho_i + {}_pt_{ci} = 0. \tag{11.31}$$

If we further assume that

$$_{pq}T_i = {}_{pq}\tau_i \cdot {}_{pq}x_j, \tag{11.32}$$

then we get the objective function as

$$\int \sum_p \sum_q \sum_i \sum_j {}_{pq}\tau_j \cdot {}_{pq}x_i \cdot x_j. \tag{11.33}$$

So for the Euler condition we get the new equation

$$\frac{\partial F}{\partial {}_{pq}x_i} = \sum_j {}_{pq}\tau_j \cdot {}_{pq}x_i - {}_p\lambda_i + {}_{pq}\eta_i = 0. \tag{11.34}$$

This thus, relates the Lagrange multipliers to the flow variable $_{pq}x_i$. Otherwise there is no change in the programme.

It is interesting to note that the solution in the present formulation is independent of the time path of x, c and $\dot{x}$, and only lays down some conditions for the time path of the shadow value system.

TIME-OPTIMAL PROBLEM

An important class of locational problems in this area may be formulated as follows. Given a number of regions with different production functions and given that the regional economics are to grow from a certain initial state to an assigned terminal state, determine the policy to be followed regarding location which minimises the time taken to reach the terminal state. These problems are most amenable to treatment by Pontryagins' Maximum Principle.

A basic assumption is that nature of the production functions do not change over time. Kurz (1965) has analysed a similar problem. We may extend this to a two-sector, two-region case. We confine our present discussion to the problem of switching without going into the problem of the trajectory.

Define an economy in two sectors, capital goods and consumer's goods, and two regions (i.e. $i = 1, 2; j = 1, 2$). Let $_ik_j$ be the capital employed in region i, sector j, $_il_j$ be the labour employed in region i, sector j.

Let the production functions be defined as

$$_iQ_j = {}_iF_j({}_ik_j\,{}_il_j) = {}_il_j \cdot {}_i\bar{F}_j \left(\frac{{}_ik_j}{{}_il_j} \right), \tag{11.35}$$

with assumptions of homogeneity and concavity.

$$_i\bar{F}'_j > 0 \quad (_i\bar{F}''_j < 0), \tag{11.36}$$

$$\bar{F}_i(0) = 0 \quad (\bar{F}'_i(0) = \infty), \tag{11.37}$$

$$\bar{F}_i(\infty) = \infty \quad (\bar{F}'_i(\infty) = 0). \tag{11.38}$$

Further let
$$\sum_i \sum_j {}_il_j = l = l_0 e^{nt}. \tag{11.39}$$

It is assumed that there is no depreciation.
Define

$$_i\bar{k}_j = \frac{_ik_j}{l}, \tag{11.40}$$

$$\frac{_ik_j}{_1F_1 + {}_2F_1} = {}_iu_j, \tag{11.41}$$

$$\frac{_il_j}{l} = {}_iv_j, \tag{11.42}$$

$$\sum_i \sum_j {}_ik_j = {}_1F_1 + {}_2F_1 = \text{total capital formation.} \tag{11.43}$$

$_iu_j$ represents the position where total investment is employed in the jth sector (capital or consumers' goods) in the ith region. We therefore also have
$$\sum_i \sum_j {}_iu_j = 1, \quad \sum_i \sum_j {}_iv_j = 1. \tag{11.44}$$

We have on differentiating $_i\bar{k}_j$

$$_i\dot{\bar{k}}_j = {}_i\bar{k}_j \frac{_ik_j}{_ik_j} - {}_i\bar{k}_j \cdot \frac{l}{l}. \tag{11.45}$$

Making further substitution we get

$$_i\dot{\bar{k}}_j = \frac{_i\bar{k}_j ({}_1F_1 + {}_2F_1) {}_iu_j}{_ik_j} - {}_i\bar{k}_j \cdot \frac{l}{l}.$$

Substituting again, we get

$$_i\dot{\bar{k}}_j = \frac{_i\bar{k}_j({}_1l_1 \cdot {}_1\bar{F}_1 + {}_2l_1 \cdot {}_2\bar{F}_1)}{_ik_j \cdot} {}_iu_j - {}_i\bar{k}_j \cdot \frac{l}{l}$$

$$= \frac{_i\bar{k}_j({}_1v_1 \cdot {}_1\bar{F}_1 \cdot l + {}_2v_1 \cdot {}_2\bar{F}_1 \cdot l) {}_iu_j}{_ik_j} - {}_i\bar{k}_j \cdot \frac{l}{l}.$$

Rewriting the set we get

$$_1\dot{\bar{k}}_1 = ({}_1v_1 \cdot {}_1\bar{F}_1 + {}_2v_1 \cdot {}_2\bar{F}_1) {}_1u_1 - {}_1\bar{k}_1 . n,$$

$$_2\dot{\bar{k}}_1 = ({}_1v_1 \cdot {}_1\bar{F}_1 + {}_2v_1 \cdot {}_2\bar{F}_1) {}_2u_1 - {}_2\bar{k}_1 . n,$$

$$_1\dot{\bar{k}}_2 = ({}_1v_1 \cdot {}_1\bar{F}_1 + {}_2v_1 \cdot {}_2\bar{F}_1) {}_1u_2 - {}_1\bar{k}_2 . n,$$

$$_2\dot{\bar{k}}_2 = ({}_1v_1 \cdot {}_1\bar{F}_1 + {}_2v_1 \cdot {}_2\bar{F}_1) (1 - {}_1u_1 - {}_1u_2 - {}_2u_1) - {}_2\bar{k}_2 . n.$$

We may now state the problem as follows.
Minimise

$$D = \int_0^T F(_ik_j, {}_iu_j, {}_iv_j, t)\, dt,$$

where $F = 1$, satisfying the differential equations listed above and further satisfying the condition that if T is the terminal point we have

$$_ik_j(T) = {}_iX_j(T), \tag{11.46}$$

$$_ik_j(O) = {}_iX_j(O). \tag{11.47}$$

We can formulate the Hamiltonian H as follows:

$$H = (_1\nu_1 \cdot {}_1\bar{F}_1 + {}_2\nu_1 \cdot {}_2\bar{F}_1)\,[_1\psi_1 \cdot {}_1u_1 + {}_2\psi_1 \cdot {}_2u_1 + {}_1\psi_2 \cdot {}_1u_2$$

$$+ {}_2\psi_2(1 - {}_1u_1 - {}_2u_1 - {}_1u_2)] - [_1\psi_1 \cdot {}_1\bar{k}_1 \cdot n + {}_2\psi_1 \cdot {}_2\bar{k}_1 \cdot n$$

$$+ {}_1\psi_2 \cdot {}_1\bar{k}_2 \cdot n + {}_2\psi_2(1 - {}_1u_1 - {}_2u_1 - {}_1u_2)\,{}_2\bar{k}_2 \cdot n]. \tag{11.48}$$

By the Maximum Principle if $_1\psi_1 > 0$ and also $> {}_2\psi_1$, or $_1\psi_2$ or $_2\psi_2$ we have $_1u_1 = 1$, if we also have $_1\bar{F}_1 > {}_2\bar{F}_1$ then $_1\nu_1 = 1$, and so on.

Under given assumptions we can now discuss one possible strategy as an example. When $_1u_1 = 1$ and $_1\nu_1 = 1$ we have,

$$\left.\begin{aligned}
\frac{d\,_1\psi_1}{dt} &= -{}_1\psi_1 \cdot ({}_1\bar{F}_1' - n), \\[4pt]
\frac{d\,_2\psi_1}{dt} &= -{}_2\psi_1(-n), \\[4pt]
\frac{d\,_1\psi_2}{dt} &= -{}_1\psi_2(-n), \\[4pt]
\frac{d\,_2\psi_2}{dt} &= -{}_2\psi_2(-n).
\end{aligned}\right\} \tag{11.49}$$

We have for the trajectory of $_ik_j$,

$$\left.\begin{aligned}
\frac{d\,_1\bar{k}_1}{dt} &= ({}_1\bar{F}_1 - {}_1\bar{k}_1 \cdot n), \\[4pt]
\frac{d\,_2\bar{k}_1}{dt} &= -{}_2\bar{k}_1 \cdot n, \\[4pt]
\frac{d\,_1\bar{k}_2}{dt} &= -{}_1\bar{k}_2 \cdot n, \\[4pt]
\frac{d\,_2\bar{k}_2}{dt} &= -{}_2\bar{k}_2 \cdot n.
\end{aligned}\right\} \tag{11.50}$$

During the period t_0 to t^* say, when $_1u_1 = 1$ and $_1v_1 = 1$, all new investment goes into the first sector and all the labour goes into the first sector. Since it is assumed that L grows exponentially at the rate of n, the capital growth-path in all sectors other than the first will decline per unit of labour at the same rate, as no new investment takes place in other sectors.

In the first sector all new capital goes into the first sector and therefore the capital per unit of output grows at the rate at which output of capital goods per unit grows in sector 1 of region 1. But since labour is also growing exponentially at the rate n this depresses the rate of growth, g, capital per labour unit in this sector, by an amount equal to the rate of growth of labour, x, the capital per unit of labour in the same sector. This is due to the absorption by new labour of capital goods in their turn in sector 1.

As may be seen, the situation outlined here is an oversimplified one. But in such oversimplified situations the rather extreme measures, which are generally recommended in the optimal solutions arrived at by using Pontryagin's methods, are clearly revealed.

There is no switch from $_1u_1$ or $_2u_1$ to $_1u_2$ or $_2u_2$ during this period. Thus the problem of capital accumulation is only for capital goods between regions 1 and 2.

The problem thus emphasises the basic feature of the optimal strategy – go all out for the region where the highest absolute rate of growth is possible in capital goods, stop at the point where the rate of growth in the capital goods sector of the other region becomes higher. The whole of the investment should then be shifted to the other region. If the target has already been achieved in the more efficient region, the shift will take place earlier.

THE MAXIMUM PRINCIPLE WITH A SIMPLER PRODUCTION FUNCTION

A case of the application of the Maximum Principle with a simpler production function is discussed below.

Let the production functions be

$$_iQ_j = {_iF_j}(_ik_j). \tag{11.51}$$

Defining 'u's as before
$$_iu_j = \frac{_ik_j}{_1F_1 + {_2F_1}}, \tag{11.52}$$

we have again
$$\sum_i \sum_j {_iu_j} = 1, \tag{11.53}$$

$$\sum_i \sum_j {_ik_j} = {_1F_1} + {_2F_1}, \tag{11.54}$$

We have as before

$$\begin{rcases} {}_1\dot{k}_1 = ({}_1F_1 + {}_2F_1)_1 u_1, \\ {}_2\dot{k}_1 = ({}_1F_1 + {}_2F_1) \, {}_1u_2, \\ {}_1\dot{k}_2 = ({}_1F_1 + {}_2F_1) \, {}_1u_2, \\ {}_2\dot{k}_2 = (1 - {}_1u_1 - {}_1u_2 - {}_2u_1)({}_1F_1 + {}_2F_1). \end{rcases} \quad (11.55)$$

This again gives us for the Hamiltonian

$$H = ({}_1F_1 + {}_2F_1)\left[{}_1\psi_1 \cdot {}_1u_1 + {}_2\psi_1 \cdot {}_2u_1 + {}_1\psi_2 \cdot {}_1u_2 \right. \\ \left. + {}_2\psi_2(1 - {}_1u_1 - {}_2u_1 - {}_1u_2)\right] \quad (11.56)$$

If ${}_i u_j^*$ are optimal policies we have by the Maximum Principle,

$$\frac{d\,{}_i\psi_j}{dt} = -\frac{\partial H}{\partial\,{}_i k_j}$$

$$= -\frac{\partial}{\partial\,{}_i k_j}\left[\sum_i\sum_j {}_i\psi_j \cdot {}_i u_j^*({}_1F_1 + {}_2F_1)\right]$$

or, $${}_i\psi_j = \int\left[-\frac{\partial}{\partial\,{}_i k_j}\left(\Sigma\Sigma\,{}_i\psi_j \cdot {}_i u_j^*({}_1F_1 + {}_2F_1)\right)\right]dt \quad (11.57)$$

also, $$\frac{d\,{}_i k_j}{dt} = \frac{\partial H}{\partial\,{}_i\psi_j}$$

$$= \frac{\partial}{\partial\,{}_i\psi_j}\left[\sum_i\sum_j {}_i\psi_j \cdot {}_i u_j^* \cdot ({}_1F_1 + {}_2F_1)\right]$$

$$= \Sigma\Sigma\,{}_i u_j^*({}_1F_1 + {}_2F_1)$$

or, $${}_i k_j = \int\left[\sum_i\sum_j {}_i u_j^*({}_1F_1 + {}_2F_1)\right]dt. \quad (11.58)$$

It is also given that

$${}_i k_j(0) = {}_i\chi_j,$$

$${}_i k_j(T) = {}_i\bar{\chi}_j \quad (11.59)$$

while the trajectory of ${}_i\psi_j$ is rather complicated the trajectory of the ${}_i u_j$ is clearly defined. This trajectory once more lays down the rule that the entire new capital stock must be invested in the industry and region with the largest ${}_i\psi_j$, since H is maximised for the largest ${}_i\psi_j$ when the corresponding ${}_i u_j = 1$.

A MODEL WITH A LINEAR PRODUCTION FUNCTION

To bring out clearly the implications of the controls, ${}_i u_j$, and the nature of the possible switch, we consider a simple linear production function as follows:

$$ {}_i Q_j = {}_i b_j \cdot {}_i k_j, \quad (11.60)$$

$$_iu_j = \frac{_ik_j}{_1b_1 \cdot _1k_1 + _2b_1 \cdot _2k_1} \qquad (11.61)$$

or,

$$_i\dot{k}_j = {}_iu_j(_1b_1 \cdot _1k_1 + _1b_1 \cdot _2k_1), \qquad (11.62)$$

$$\Sigma\Sigma_iu_j = 1,$$

with,

$$\left.\begin{array}{l} _ik_j(0) = {}_ix_j, \\ _ik_j(T) = {}_i\bar{x}_j \end{array}\right\} \qquad (11.63)$$

i and j as before are considered for two regions and two sectors only and the integral to be minimised is

$$\int_0^T F(_ik_j, \, _i\dot{k}_j, \, _iu_j)\, dt. \qquad (11.64)$$

The Hamiltonian H may be written as

$$\begin{aligned} H = (_1b_1 \cdot _1k_1 + _2b_1 \cdot _2k_1)\,[(_1\psi_1 - _2\psi_2)\,(_1u_1) \\ + (_2\psi_1 - _2\psi_2)_2u_1 + (_1\psi_2 - _2\psi_2)\,_2u_2 + _2\psi_2]. \end{aligned} \qquad (11.65)$$

By the Maximum Principle the consistency conditions give the trajectories of $_i\psi_j$ as follows:

$$\left.\begin{array}{l} \dfrac{d_1\psi_1}{dt} = {}_1b_1[_1u_1^*(_1\psi_1 - _2\psi_2) + _2u_1^*(_2\psi_1 - _2\psi_2) \\ \qquad + _1u_2^*(_1\psi_2 - _2\psi_2)], \\[2mm] \dfrac{d_2\psi_1}{dt} = -_2b_1[_1u_1^*(_1\psi_1 - _2\psi_2) + _2u_1^*(_2\psi_1 - _2\psi_2) \\ \qquad + _1u_2^*(_1\psi_2 - _2\psi_2)], \\[2mm] \dfrac{d_1\psi_2}{dt} = 0, \quad \dfrac{d_2\psi_2}{dt} = 0 \end{array}\right\} \qquad (11.66)$$

if u^* are optimal policies the trajectories of $_ik_j$ are given as below:

$$\left.\begin{array}{l} \dfrac{d_1k_1}{dt} = {}_1u_1^*(_1b_1 \cdot _1k_1 + _2b_1 \cdot _2k_1), \\[2mm] \dfrac{d_2k_2}{dt} = {}_2u_1^*(_1b_1 \cdot _1k_1 + _2b_1 \cdot _2k_1), \\[2mm] \dfrac{d_1k_2}{dt} = {}_1u_2^*(_1b_1 \cdot _1k_1 + _2b_1 \cdot _2k_1), \\[2mm] \dfrac{d_2k_2}{dt} = (1 - {}_1u_1^* - {}_2u_1^* - {}_1u_1^*)(_1b_1 \cdot _1k_1 + _2b_1 \cdot _2k_1) \end{array}\right\} \qquad (11.67)$$

and the initial and terminal restrictions are:

$$\left.\begin{array}{l} _ik_j(0) = {}_ix_j \\ _ik_j(T) = {}_i\bar{x}_j \end{array}\right\} \text{ (given).} \qquad (11.68)$$

The trajectories of $_ik_j$ must satisfy both initial and terminal conditions but the trajectories of $_i\psi_j$ have no conditions attached to them.

To solve for the time-path of $_i\psi_j$ therefore, initial values of $_i\psi_j$ must be chosen in such a way as to be consistent with both the initial and terminal conditions on $_ik_j$.

There is no standard technique for doing this but computerised methods can be developed for handling such problems.

From the nature of the function H we can see that $_iu_j$'s are either 1 or 0 and the optimal control will pass from a sector of any region to another and the entire capital output will be channelled into one sector of a specific region at a time. One can work out the probable nature of the trajectory under some simple assumptions regarding $_i\psi_j(0)$. Assume for example,

$$_1\psi_1(0) - {_2\psi_2(0)} > {_2\psi_1(0)} - {_2\psi_2(0)}$$

and

$$> {_1\psi_2(0)} - {_2\psi_2(0)}$$

and also > 0.

We have,

$$H = \left(_1b_1._1k_1 + {_2b_1._2k_1}\right)\left[\left(_1\psi_1 - {_2\psi_2}\right)_1u_1 + \left(_2\psi_1 - {_2\psi_2}\right)_2u_1 \right.$$
$$\left. + \left(_1\psi_2 - {_2\psi_2}\right)_1u_2 + {_2\psi_2}\right] \tag{11.69}$$

then for Maximum H, $_1u_1 = 1$. $_2u_1$, $_1u_2$ are zeros and we have,

$$\left.\begin{aligned}
\frac{d\,_1\psi_1}{dt} &= -{_1b_1._1\psi_1}, \\[4pt]
\frac{d\,_2\psi_1}{dt} &= -{_2b_1._1\psi_1}, \\[4pt]
\frac{d\,_1\psi_2}{dt} &= 0, \\[4pt]
\frac{d\,_2\psi_2}{dt} &= 0
\end{aligned}\right\} \tag{11.70}$$

and we have for $_ik_j$,

$$\left.\begin{aligned}
\frac{d\,_1k_1}{dt} &= {_1b_1._1k_1} + {_2b_1._2k_1}, \\[4pt]
\frac{d\,_2k_1}{dt} &= 0, \quad \frac{d\,_1k_2}{dt} = 0, \quad \frac{d\,_2k_2}{dt} = 0.
\end{aligned}\right\} \tag{11.71}$$

Solving for the trajectory of $_1\psi_1$ and $_2\psi_1$ we get,

$$_1\psi_1 = {_1\psi_1(0)} \exp\left[-{_1b_1}.t\right] \tag{11.72}$$

and

$$_2\psi_1 = {_1\psi_1(0)}._2b_1\left(\frac{1}{_1b_1}.\exp\left[-{_1b_1}.t\right] + 1\right) \tag{11.73}$$

at $t = 0$,
$$_1\psi_1 = {}_1\psi_1(0),$$
$$_2\psi_1 = {}_1\psi_1(0) \cdot {}_2 b_1\left(\frac{1}{{}_1 b_1} + 1\right).$$
$$(11.74)$$

There is thus a consistency condition on the initial situation which has implications on our assumption about the initial $_i\psi_j$'s.

Coming to the trajectory of $_i k_j$ the rule that all new capital goods are to flow into the first sector over the interval holds, so that we have

$$\frac{d_1 k_1}{dt} = {}_1 b_1 \cdot {}_1 k_1 + {}_2 b_1 \cdot {}_2 k_1(0),$$
$$\frac{d_2 k_1}{dt} = 0 \quad \text{or,} \quad {}_2 k_1 = {}_2 k_1(0).$$
$$(11.75)$$

Solving the equation, for the trajectory of $_1 k_1$, we get,

$$_1 k_1 = \frac{{}_1\rho_1}{{}_1 b_1} \exp\left({}_1 b_1 \cdot t\right) - \frac{{}_2 b_1 \cdot {}_2 k_1(0)}{{}_1 b_1} \qquad (11.76)$$

at $t = 0$
$$_1 k_1(0) = \frac{{}_1\rho_1}{{}_1 b_1} - \frac{{}_2 b_1}{{}_1 b_1} \cdot {}_2 k_1(0), \qquad (11.77)$$

where $_1\rho_1$ is an arbitrary constant.

There is thus a restriction on the initial condition of the two capital goods sector.

We may now briefly consider the switching from the first sector of the first region $(_1 u_1)$.

If at t^* there is a switch to say $_2 u_1$ then,

$$_1\psi_1(t^*) = {}_2\psi_1(t^*)$$

or,
$$\exp\left[-{}_1 b_1 \cdot t^*\right] = \frac{{}_2 b_1}{{}_1 b_1} \cdot \exp\left[-{}_1 b_1 \cdot t^*\right] + {}_2 b_1. \qquad (11.78)$$

Since we assumed to begin with that $_1\psi_1 > {}_2\psi_1$, then for a switch we must have

$$\frac{d_2\psi_1}{dt} > \frac{d_1\psi_1}{dt} \qquad (11.79)$$

or,
$$-{}_2 b_1 \cdot {}_1\psi_1 > -{}_1 b_1 \cdot {}_1\psi_1$$

or,
$$_2 b_1 < {}_1 b_1. \qquad (11.80)$$

Thus a set of consistency conditions in this simple case does restrict the initial values and the trajectories in specific ways.

The possibilities of making more meaningful models on this line for regional allocation, with certain minimum rates of growth for specific sectors built in to avoid extreme situations, may have important applications in this kind of problem for India and other developing countries.

GENERAL COMMENTS

In all the various sophistications discussed above the question arises as to what extent numerically computable formulations can be made with numerical answers. For problems classed in integer programming or quadratic programming the transition to numerical models may be difficult, but not impossible. Given a large enough computing unit, such problems can indeed be put into numerical forms, giving us more realistic insight into various features of the optimal location problem.

In the case of the variational approach including Pontryagin the answers must, even if numerically formulated, be a little different. The main interest in these cases, assuming that suitable integrals can be framed numerically, lies in the nature of the trajectory of the path which the regional investments should take and the switch from investment in one set of regions to another which will minimise the time needed for growth. Though difficult, such numerical formulations can possibly be made with varying simplifications and solved. These solutions will give us new insight into the long-term problems.

APPENDIX TO CHAPTER 5

The empirical implementation of the model in Chapter 5 is based on data relating to the Indian Union in 1954. A regional input–output table has been used as the basis from which the present aggregation has been done. The sectors relate to coal, sugar, jute, cotton, cement, iron and steel and 'others'. Table A5.1 gives the input–output coefficients

TABLE A5.1.

Sector	1	2	3	4	5	6	7
				Region 1			
1	(0.064001)	0.000315	0.1533603	0.001806	0.008150	0.019984	0.00323
2		(0.001093)					
3					0.000404		
4				(0.089991)	0.003717	0.002320	
5		0.003347	0.137262	0.000600	(0.00431)	0.063343	0.00040
6						(0.110191)	0.00973
				Region 2			
1	(0.064001)	0.003092	0.114234	0.001352	0.012826	0.110191	0.00150
2		(0.030068)					0.00023
3					0.000337		
4				(0.061454)	0.000675		
5		0.018675	0.131862	0.000546	(0.000675)	0.001609	0.00034
6						(0.120500)	0.000384
				Region 3			
1	(0.063999)	0.001060	0.153603	0.005121	0.040072	0.068837	0.00058
2		(0.018354)					0.00006
3							
4				(0.001985)			
5		0.006753	0.135679	0.001135	(0.010173)		0.00015
6					0.522451		0.00193
				Region 5			
1		0.013340	0.052231	0.001451	0.024362	0.093165	0.00055
2		(0.005780)					0.00016
3							
4				(0.208800)	0.001070		
5		0.0004086	0.134640	0.001197		0.017549	0.00027
6						(0.366194)	0.00109
				Region 6			
1	(0.007388)	0.001343	0.153603	0.012177		0.004938	0.00260
2	0.030631	(0.005570)					0.0004
3							
4				(0.540219)			
5	0.042458	0.007721	0.137262	0.003599	(0.000177)		0.00067
6					0.507497		0.00038

The original table considers sixteen sectors and five regions. In the present model the dimensions have been reduced for preliminary experimentation.

TABLE A5.2. *Definitions of the regions*

Region 1	Region 2	Region 3	Region 4	Region 5
West Bengal	Bihar	Punjab Madhya Pradesh Delhi	Madras	Bombay
Orissa	Uttar Pradesh	Rajasthan Pepsu Ajmir Himachal Pradesh	Andhra Mysore	Saurashtra
Assam		Vindhya Pradesh	Kerala	

Since we are considering only a few sectors explicitly, the balance relation makes it imperative that a sector comprising all the other industries be considered exogenous along with
final demand or be included as a composite group. Table A5.3 gives the transport costs and
the labour costs for the sectors in each region.

TABLE A5.3. *Transport cost from one region to another per Leontief unit (in Rs.)*

Region	1	2	3	4	5
			Coal		
1	0.9872	1.8972	3.0272	2.8972	3.2872
2	1.9269	0.4169	2.3169	3.5669	2.8269
3	2.8856	2.1456	0.2456	3.6556	2.4156
4	2.8886	3.6286	3.7886	0.3786	2.6386
5	2.9000	3.4100	2.1700	2.2600	0
			Sugar		
1	0.0953	0.1290	0.1543	0.1514	0.1602
2	0.1221	0.0884	0.1310	0.1588	0.1423
3	0.0910	0.0746	0.0320	0.1083	0.0805
4	0.1410	0.1553	0.1612	0.0849	0.1355
5	0.1397	0.1287	0.1233	0.1254	0.0748
			Cement		
1	0.1218	7.2318	12.5618	11.9418	13.8118
2	7.1939	0.0839	9.0639	14.9239	11.4539
3	12.5332	9.0732	0.0932	16.1732	10.3132
4	11.9037	14.9237	16.1637	0.0837	10.7437
5	13.7980	11.4780	10.3280	10.7680	0.1080
			Cotton		
1	0.2503	0.2570	0.2620	0.2614	0.2632
2	0.2087	0.2020	0.2105	0.2160	0.2127
3	0.2390	0.2358	0.2273	0.2425	0.2369
4	0.1846	0.1875	0.1887	0.1735	0.1835
5	0.2642	0.2620	0.2609	0.2613	0.2513

TABLE A5.3. (*cont.*)

Region	1	2	3	4	5
			Jute		
1	0.1837	0.2005	0.2130	0.2116	0.2160
2	0.2563	0.2395	0.2607	0.2745	0.2664
3	0.3109	0.3088	0.2876	0.3255	0.3117
4	0.2281	0.2352	0.2381	0.2002	0.2253
5	0.0323	0.0269	0.0241	0.0251	—
			Iron and steel		
1	0.2511	0.3111	0.3736	0.3675	0.3858
2	0.2816	0.2116	0.3000	0.3578	0.3236
3	0.2956	0.2615	0.1731	0.3315	0.2737
4	0.3159	0.3457	0.3579	0.1995	0.3045
5	0.3808	0.3581	0.3467	0.3511	0.2461

		Labour cost per Leontief unit			
Region	Coal	Sugar	Cement	Cotton	Jute	Iron
1	0.3872	0.0953	0.1218	0.2503	0.1837	0.2511
2	0.4169	0.0884	0.0839	0.2020	0.2395	0.2116
3	0.2456	0.0320	0.0932	0.2273	0.2876	0.1731
4	0.3786	0.0849	0.0837	0.1735	0.2002	0.1995
5	—	0.0748	0.1008	0.2513	—	0.2461

THE PRICE PROBLEM

Before going on to the other basic tables it is necessary to clear up the problem of price variations and its effect on the interregional tables. The problem arises because of local variations in price of the same commodity in different regions. The input–output flow tables compiled from the usual official statistics generally reflect local costs. But the interregional commodity flow tables were in physical quantities and the transportation costs are usually given in money per physical unit, i.e., they are more or less uniform from region to region in India. To convert the whole model into the same unit we have to reduce the costs either to physical quantities or to a common Leontief unit based on a suitable price system.

To do this we make the following assumptions. In most regions, the input–output-flow tables reflect the local costs of inputs and the value of the product at local prices. Let us assume that the inputs are valued in terms of the prices charged by the biggest producers or, if there is more than one big producer, by an average. This means that any region using a commodity which it mainly imports will pay a price for this input determined by a large producer of the input. Thus inputs are assumed to be in dominant all-India prices. Small producers who use them pay what the big producers of these commodities declare to be their price. The outputs, however, are in local prices, and have to be transformed into all-Indian prices by a suitable index. This means in effect that input values are accepted as they are, but outputs are expressed in terms of all-India ruling prices.

The consequence of using this method is that the coefficients of any big producer of a commodity will not be changed. His inputs are in all-India prices and his outputs are also in dominant all-India prices. For small producers output values will be changed, leading to changes in the local coefficients. Table A5.4 gives the local output prices and the all-India prices assumed in the current study.

TABLE A5.4. *Regional prices per tonne various commodities with corresponding all-India prices*
(*in Rs.*)

| Commodities | Regions | | | | | All-India |
	1	2	3	4	5	
Coal	15.27	13.67	14.88	21.52	—	14.41
Sugar	680.60	619.81	680.60	697.90	740.66	664.69
Cement	—	—	—	—	—	—
Cotton	3699.20	2662.40	2956.40	3238.40	3302.40	3237.26
Jute	1294.69	1181.20	1113.42	1153.59	—	1294.69
Iron and steel	279.50	310.52	472.31	473.01	422.14	429.89

Table A5.5 gives figures for final demand and 'other output', as estimated for sectors not included in these six.

TABLE A 5.5. (*in crores of Rs.*)

| Sectors | Regions | | | | |
	1	2	3	4	5
Coal	3.0	5.0	3.0	1.9	1.5
Sugar	18.6	79.8	36.2	46.1	32.3
Cement	—	—	—	—	—
Cotton	110.5	205.8	121.4	175.8	105.1
Jute	115.2	—	—	—	—
Iron and steel	14.6	24.5	—	—	—
Other output	1126.4	1774.2	1702.4	1293.4	887.2

As may be seen, it has been assumed that cement is not included in final demand, except in region 2 where there are some exports. Jute is not in final demand except in region 1, as it is either exported or has inter-industrial use, and it is exported only from region 1. Similarly 'iron and steel' is exported as final output only from regions 1 and 2.

The transport constraints (T_{pq}) are given in tonnes in Table A5.6.

TABLE A5.6.

| Sector | Regions (in 1000 tonnes) | | | | |
	1	2	3	4	5
1	×	1971	1012	227	136
2	4458	×	590	429	1010
3	27	329	×	691	1642
4	30	22	41	×	×
5	22	37	222	49	×

These constraints were determined on the basis of the present actual load carried and other considerations.

× Indicates that particular flows were not provided for.

APPENDIX TO CHAPTERS 6–9

THE REGIONS

The states were aggregated regionally into six territorial groups: the states of Assam and West Bengal as region 1; Bihar and Orissa as Region 2; Uttar Pradesh and Madhya Pradesh as region 3 ; Punjab and Delhi as region 4; Maharastra, Gujrat and Rajasthan as region 5 and the remaining states of South India as region 6. The state of Jammu and Kashmir and such Chief Commissioners' states as Manipur, Tripura and Pondicherry were not taken into account. The economic activities of a region were assumed to take place at a specific point where the region has shown a high concentration of economic activities over a long period. The representative points for the six regions are as follows: Calcutta in region 1, Jamshedpur in region 2, Bhopal in region 3, Jullundhur in region 4, Bombay in region 5 and Bangalore in region 6.

In this study all foreign exports have been assumed to pass through one of the three major ports – Calcutta, Bombay and Madras.

THE SECTORS

Coal includes coke (both hard and soft). The iron and steel industry as defined here encompasses only the *Annual Survey of Industries*, (ASI) classification of the iron and steel industry. We have omitted the ferro–alloys industry because of its small locational impact on the growth of other important industries. The iron and steel industry therefore includes: iron and steel (metal), castings and forgings, structurals, pipes and tubes.

To keep the problem reasonably small for the computer different disaggregations are used in the study in different kinds of analysis. Thus in part of the analysis iron and steel has been split up into two groups. We have aggregated the four groups mentioned above into two broad groups, iron and steel (1) and iron and steel (2). Iron and steel (1) consists of all iron and steel items, except bars and rods, included in the iron and steel (metal) group of the ASI classification. Bars and rods and the remaining three groups (castings and forgings, structurals and pipes and tubes) comprise iron and steel (2). Only large integrated iron and steel plants produce iron and steel (1) of course, but these also produce iron and steel bars and rods as well. In 1960–1 more than half of the iron and steel output came from units other than the large integrated iron and steel plants and was included in iron and steel (2). In another model iron and steel was considered as one sector ,while engineering was broken up into two, as described in the next paragraph.

The engineering industry by our definition is synonymous with three major ASI industry groups – electrical equipment, non-electrical equipment and transport equipment – covering altogether fifty industries. Engineering industries were put under the head of engineering (1) or engineering (2), according to whether their expenditure on coal, coke and iron and steel materials was more or less than 40 per cent of their total consumption of materials. This new type of classification of engineering industries was done deliberately in order to study the impact of sectoral interdependence on the choice of location. The coverage of these two subgroups is indicated below.

Engineering (1) – manufacture of ships and other power-driven vessels, manufacture of motor vehicles, manufacture of motor cycles and bicycles, equipment for generation, transmission and distribution of electricity, electric fans, electric furnaces and manufacture of electrical machines and appliances, textile machinery, jute machinery, tea machinery, paper machinery, mining machinery, earthmoving machinery, size-reduction pumps, fire-fighting equipment, ball, roller and tapered bearings, tractors and harvesters, sewing and knitting machines, manufacture of machinery other than electrical machinery – also, telephones, railway locomotives, refrigeration plants, typewriters and duplicators, air-conditioners and refrigerators.

Engineering (2) – railway rolling stock, electric motors, household appliances (electric irons, heaters, etc.), telegraph equipment, internal combustion engines, sugar machinery, metallurgical and pharmaceutical machinery, chemical machinery, construction machinery, oil mill machinery, rice, dal and flour-mill machinery, conveying equipment, buckets, elevators, ship hoists, etc., power-driven pumps, machine tools, agricultural implements, weighing machines and boat-building.

The two main modes of transport used by the industries in which we are interested are rail and road. Of course, some domestic movement of coal and iron and steel materials also takes place through coastal shipping. But we have assumed that the railways and roads are the only two modes of transport available to our producers and consumers.

INTER-INDUSTRY INPUT COEFFICIENTS

Dhar (1965) constructed an input–output table for India for the year 1954–5. The Economics Division of the Planning Commission has an input–output table for the Indian economy covering twenty-eight sectors for the year 1959. Manne and Rudra (1965) have also constructed a thirty-sector inter-industry transaction table for India for 1960–1. In our construction of separate input-coefficient tables for the six regions of our study, we depended mainly on the ASI 1961, though we have whenever necessary used the other sources mentioned.

No industry except coal (including coke) contributes to the production of all six industries. Transport contributes to four, all except itself and coal. Transport as an input of an industry here only covers the transportation services required for carrying its raw materials. It does not include transport from the factories to the consumers. Strictly speaking, from this angle the coal industry should have a transportation input through coke; coal, the raw material of coke, has to be carried from the mines to the cokeries and coke-oven plants. We have taken account of the transportation involved in the carrying of coal from mines to the five coke-oven plants attached to the steel plants in the transportation coefficient of iron and steel (1). The combined output of the remaining coke-oven plant at Sindhri and the cokeries then becomes very small and the demand on transportation services they make is small and can be ignored. Iron and steel (1) and engineering (1) both provide inputs for three industries: the former for iron and steel (2), engineering (1) and engineering (2); the latter for coal, engineering (1) and engineering (2). Iron and steel (2) and engineering (2) offer inputs only to engineering (1) and engineering (2).

INTER-SECTORAL COEFFICIENT FOR COAL

The *Annual Report* of the Chief Inspector of Mines is the relevant source for this information, but it gives only all-India figures. From the *Annual Report* of 1960 we obtain the amount of coal utilised for coke-making at the collieries, as well as the amount of coal consumed within the collieries for boilers, attached power houses, etc. The corresponding outputs of coke and coal are also obtained from the same source. From this the self-consumption coefficient of the sector is determined, with suitable prices specified on an all-India basis.

ENGINEERING (1) INPUT COEFFICIENT OF COAL

This is another coefficient for which independent regional estimates could not be obtained. The same coefficient has been made to hold good for all the six coal-producing regions, except Delhi–Punjab. This coefficient has been adopted from Manne and Rudra's (1965) inter-industry transaction table, with a slight amendment for price changes between 1959–60 and 1960–1. Manne and Rudra, however, do not classify engineering into engineering (1) and engineering (2).

COAL INPUT COEFFICIENT OF IRON AND STEEL (1)

The production of iron and steel products of type 1 is carried on in three main regions – in region 1 by Hindusthan Steel Limited, (HSL), Durgapur, and Indian Iron and Steel Company (IISCO), Burnpur; in region 2 by Tata Iron and Steel Company (TISCO), Jamshedpur and Hindusthan Steel Limited at Rourkela; in region 3 by Hindusthan Steel Limited, Bhilai. In region 6 before the mid-1960s the Mysore Iron and Steel Ltd, Bhadravati used to produce some iron and steel (1) products. But since 1964 the factory has been converted into a unit specialising in the production of tool, alloy and special steel, which in terms of our classification are iron and steel (2) items. If in the not-too-distant future the government sets up additional steel plants, the south will present a strong case in favour of such sites as Salem, Vishakhapatnam. So even if region 6 is not a current producer of iron and steel (1), we should not overlook its role as a potential producer. In that capacity one can only make rough guesses about its coal input coefficient. The best guess in the existing situation seems to be to equate it with that of region 3 as neither has good coking coal deposits.

In the estimation of this coefficient for iron and steel (1), we have worked with 1962–3 figures. This is because before that the Rourkela and especially the Durgapur plant were running much below their capacity to produce ingot steel. The main source for this estimate is the *Hindusthan Steel Statistics* published by the Senior Statistical Officer, Hindusthan Steel Limited, Ranchi. This report gives 1962–3 figures of coal (both coking and non-coking) consumption and the corresponding production of finished steel for the three HSL plants as well as TISCO and IISCO, The report does not enumerate exactly how much coke was consumed by these plants during the period. In the absence of this information we have worked out the coke consumption from the coking coal figures by using a conversion factor of 0.6375. This is a rough estimate, indicating how much coke of the appropriate size for blast furnaces is available from 1 tonne of coking coal, when its volatile products and the run-over have been eliminated. (This figure is our computation. But we are grateful to the scientists of the Central Fuel Research Institute, Jeolgorath, for helpful discussions.) Because of our lack of knowledge of the grades of coking coal consumed in the coke oven, there are no firm estimates available of operating charges in the different coke-oven plants. So a uniform coke price of Rs. 60.63/-tonne was held to be valid for all regions. Non-coking coal was valued at Rs. 22.27/-tonne.

Looking at these coefficients one finds that region 1 has a much higher figure than region 2 and region 3. This is partly explained by the wasteful method of production in the HSL plant at Durgapur, but mainly by the fact that region 1 uses more unwashed coal than the others.

COAL COEFFICIENT OF IRON AND STEEL (2)

The coal and coke consumption of the three subgroups of iron and steel (2) – castings and forgings, structurals, pipes and tubes – were directly obtained from the ASI, 1961. The separation of the coal and coke consumed by the re-rollers in the iron and steel (metal) group was, however, not easily achieved. This difficulty was overcome by working out the coal and coke coefficient of re-rollers from an independent source, the *Report of the Iron and Steel Controller*. For each region the coefficient of the broad group iron and steel (2) is a weighted average of the coefficient of the re-rollers and those of the three remaining groups. The weights are, of course, the respective regional outputs.

COAL COEFFICIENT OF ENGINEERING (1) AND
ENGINEERING (2)

These coefficients are based solely on the coal and coke consumption data given in *ASI*, 1961. The corresponding output figures were also obtained from the same source.

COAL COEFFICIENT OF TRANSPORT

In the transport sector output is made synonymous with earnings. In estimating this coefficient the relevant output is the sum of gross earnings of railways and motor transport. The supplement to the *Report of the Railway Board on Indian Railways for 1964–5* (Statistical Statement) records zone-wise gross earnings and coal consumption of railways. From an unpublished report of the transport planning group we obtained the regional distribution of line-kilometres in each zone. Using these figures a set of coal norms for railways in each region was worked out. The *Report on the Material and Financial Balances* of the Perspective Planning Division works out 1960–1 gross earnings of the Indian Railways at Rs. 456.8 crores.

By accepting the regional percentage distribution of gross earnings during 1963–4, an estimate of regional earnings of railways was obtained. It was assumed that the coal norm of Indian Railways did not change significantly between 1960–1 and 1963–4. Applying the same set of coefficients as prevailed in the latter year, regional coal consumption figures of rail transport was obtained. Motor transport earnings were separately estimated for goods and passengers. An estimate of goods vehicle earnings was made from the Perspective Planning Division figures, using average capacity (in tonnes), average annual length of run and average load factor of goods vehicles. The regional availability of goods vehicles was obtained from the *Union Statistical Abstract*, 1962–3. But the problem this method posed was to find out the share of India's total motor traffic in goods during 1960–1 represented by long-distance haulage and the share of local and feeder traffic. In the absence of reliable data we accepted the Perspective Planning Division figure of 17 billion tonne-kilometres for motor traffic in goods during 1960–1. This was distributed among regions in proportion with their goods vehicle availability in 1960–1 and was valued at the 1960–1 average ratio of 10 paise per tonne-kilometre. Passenger traffic earnings of motor transport were reckoned at 56 billion tonne-kilometers during the period. It was worked out with the following assumptions – average passenger bus capacity of 40 seats, average annual run of 40,000 kilometres, average load factor of 60 per cent. The number of passenger vehicles on the road during the period was estimated as the sum of public service vehicles and miscellaneous, less others. Average earnings per passenger kilometre were 3 paise.

THE IRON AND STEEL (1) COEFFICIENT OF IRON AND STEEL (2)

The input consumption pattern of the groups (castings and forgings, structurals and pipes and tubes) is reflected in the material consumption and products and by-products table of the *ASI*. The difficulty arose once again in splitting up the re-rollers' consumption of iron and steel (1). Re-rollers use billets from the iron and steel (1) group in their production of bars and rods. The billet consumption pattern of the re-rollers was taken from the *Report of the Iron and Steel Controller*, which records the annual production of billet re-rollers as well as the quantity of billets they received annually. No time lag was assumed between supply of billets and work on them. In other words, it was assumed that the 1961–2 production of billet re-rollers came from the supply of billets they received in 1961–2. For castings and forgings, structurals, pipes and tubes, all iron and steel material consumption, except self-consumption and bars and rods, was treated as being of the iron and steel (1) variety. The input coefficient of the group as a whole was the weighted average of the coefficient of the re-rollers and that of the castings, forgings, structurals and pipes and tubes producers.

THE IRON AND STEEL (1) COEFFICIENT OF ENGINEERING (1) AND ENGINEERING (2)

These were computed from the *ASI*, 1961, which furnished all the necessary data. For iron and steel (1) the definition given in the preceding paragraph was followed and the coverage of the engineering (1) and engineering (2) industries was the same as before. The point that seems to need a comment here is the wide variability in the coefficient of the engineering (2) industries. This is due to the different component structure of the engineering (2) group of industries in the different regions.

THE IRON AND STEEL (2), ENGINEERING (1) AND ENGINEERING (2) INPUT COEFFICIENT OF ENGINEERING (1) AND ENGINEERING (2)

This group of coefficients was computed mainly on the basis of the *ASI* data for 1961. It should be pointed out here that our aim was to construct input-coefficient tables at producers' prices of 1960–1. The material consumption tables in the *ASI*, on which most of these co-efficients were based, are however in purchasers' prices. These figures therefore had to be converted into producers' prices. Manne and Rudra (1965) used a series of price deflators for 1959–60. This series was used whenever the inputs were at purchasers' prices.

THE TRANSPORTATION COEFFICIENT OF IRON AND STEEL (1)

Roy (1968) has worked out comparative estimates for 1962–3 of transport costs in the assembly of raw materials per million tonne of steel ingots for the major steel plants in India. Assuming that about 22 per cent of ingot weight is scrapped in the rolling mills (we are grateful to the Production Planning Department, HSL plant, Bhilai, for this piece of information), we work out the volume of finished steel which a one-million-tonne (ingot) plant may be expected to produce. At 1960–1 producer prices of RS. 550/tonne, the annual output of a one-million-tonne plant is worth Rs. 429 million. The transportation input coefficients for the five integrated steel plants are easily estimated on this basis. The regional coefficients are the weighted average of the plant coefficients. For example, in region 1 there are two plants, IISCO and Durgapur Steel Project (DSP), each of 1-million-tonne capacity. Here the regional average is the arithmetic average of the two. In region 2, however, while TISCO has a 2-million-tonne capacity, Rourkela is of about 1 million tonnes. Here in working out the regional coefficient TISCO was given a weight of 2 and Rourkela a weight of 1.

THE TRANSPORTATION INPUT COEFFICIENT OF IRON AND STEEL (2)

The transportation input coefficient of the castings, forgings, structurals, pipes and tubes group was estimated from *ASI*, 1961. The *Annual Survey* reports material consumption figures at purchasers' prices. All inputs reported in the material consumption table of the *ASI* were summed up (in physical units). They were than valued at producers' prices of the period; e.g. finished steel materials at Rs. 550/tonne, coal at Rs. 22.26/tonne, coke at Rs. 46.20/tonne for West Bengal and Rs. 60.63/tonne for the rest of India. The same inputs were then re-valued at purchasers' prices. The differences that resulted were used as estimates of regional transport costs for this group of industries. We took the transportation input coefficient of castings, forgings, structurals, pipes and tubes as the coefficient of iron and steel (2),

THE TRANSPORTATION INPUT COEFFICIENT OF ENGINEERING (1) AND ENGINEERING (2)

These coefficients are taken to be same for the two groups of engineering industries. The coefficient has been estimated on the basis of the planning Commission's (28×28) input–output table of the Indian Economy for 1959.

TABLE A6–9.1. *1960–1 input coefficient table (at 1960–1 producers' prices)*

	Coal	Iron and steel (1)	Iron and steel (2)	Engineering (1)	Engineering (2)	Transport
			Region 1			
Coal	0.0673	0.3060	0.0018	0.0047	0.0046	0.0233
Iron and steel (1)			0.4037	0.0260	0.1699	
Iron and steel (2)				0.0337	0.0839	
Engineering (1)	0.0336			0.0956	0.0037	
Engineering (2)				0.0287	0.1044	
Transport		0.1115	0.1414	0.0232†	0.0232†	
			Region 2			
Coal	0.0673	0.2062	0.0123	0.0073	0.0017	0.0442
Iron and steel (1)			0.5542	0.0352	0.3906	
Iron and steel (2)				0.0651	0.2100	
Engineering (1)	0.0336			0.1488	0.0032	
Engineering (2)				0.0871	0.1009	
Transport		0.0923	0.1111	0.0232†	0.0232†	
			Region 3			
Coal	0.0673	0.2141	0.0103	0.0045	0.0426	0.0428
Iron and steel (1)			0.4666	0.0348	0.0843	
Iron and steel (2)				0.0730	0.2591	
Engineering (1)	0.0336			0.1573	0.0027	
Engineering (2)				0.0882	0.0319	
Transport		0.1096	0.1259	0.0232†	0.0232†	
			Region 4			
Coal		0.0068		0.0054	0.0189	0.0334
Iron and steel (1)			0.5274	0.0439	0.2126	
Iron and steel (2)				0.1303	0.0435	
Engineering (1)				0.0876	0.0120	
Engineering (2)				0.0016	0.0073	
Transport			0.1466	0.0232†	0.0232†	

TABLE A6–9.1 (*cont.*)

	Coal	Iron and steel (1)	Iron and steel (2)	Engineering (1)	Engineering (2)	Transport
			Region 5			
Coal	0.0673		0.0005	0.0031	0.0070	0.0268
Iron and steel (1)			0.4794	0.0303	0.0885	
Iron and steel (2)				0.0416	0.1442	
Engineering (1)	0.0336			0.1870	0.0103	
Engineering (2)				0.0472	0.0458	
Transport			0.1126	0.0232†	0.0232†	
			Region 6			
Coal	0.0673	0.0583	0.0063	0.0014	0.0081	0.0283
Iron and steel (1)			0.4679	0.0347	0.0679	
Iron and steel (2)				0.0601	0.1733	
Engineering (1)	0.0336			0.1023	0.0409	
Engineering (2)				0.0778	0.0366	
Transport		0.1716	0.1298	0.0232†	0.0232†	

† All-India figure.

NOTE. The 1970–1 input coefficient tables were virtually the same as the 1961 tables. Some changes in the input coefficients were, however, made in respect of the following inter-industrial flows: engineering to engineering; coal to engineering; coal to iron and steel. These changes follow the pattern reflected by the inter-industry flow tables of 1964–5 and 1970–1 (Material and Financial Balances Tables, Perspective Planning Division).

THE COST OF PRODUCTION OF THE AVERAGE LEONTIEF UNIT

A Leontief unit is the volume of goods worth one rupee. In multi-sectoral models like the present one, output, intersectoral delivery and final demand all have to be expressed in value terms. It is imperative, therefore, that the costs of production corresponding to an inter-regional or intersectoral delivery be expressed in Leontief units.

COAL

The two main sources of information on costs of production in the coal industry were 'Costs of production of coal in India' an unpublished thesis by Sanyal (1964), and the Calcutta Stock Exchange's *Official Year Book, 1962*. Sanyal obtained from annual reports the total cost as well as depreciation, interest and other items of cost for the important collieries in West Bengal, Bihar, Madhya Pradesh, Orissa and Maharastra. Most of his data relate to the year 1961, though some also refer to 1959 and 1960. Sanyal's thesis gave us the annual raisings of coal (in value) from the important collieries in West Bengal, Bihar, Madhya, Pradesh, Orissa and Maharastra, and their respective costs. From these we estimated the Leontief unit, with adjustments for internal consumption.

TABLE A6.9.2. *Cost of production of 1 Leontief unit* (*1st estimate*)

Region	Engineering (1)	Engineering (2)	Iron and steel (1)
1	0.5011	0.4586	0.6212
2	0.6464	0.4496	0·5717
3	0.6355	0.4916	0.5650
4	0.7648	0.3832	
5	0.3963	0.4062	
6	0.5390	0.4470	

Cost of production of 1 Leontief unit (*alternative estimate*)

Region	Engineering (1)	Engineering (2)	Iron and steel (1)
1	0.6000	0.5314	0.7684
2	0.7169	0.5153	0.8532
3	0.7173	0.5592	0.8481
4	0.8335	0.4555	
5	0.4698	0.4943	
6	0.6080	0.5550	

Cost of production of 1 Leontief unit

Region	Iron and steel (2)		Coal	
	1st estimate	Alternative estimate	1st estimate	Alternative estimate
1	0.2830	0.3297	0.8483	0.8972
2	0.4725	0.5493	0.7408	0.7809
3	0.5344	0.6150	0.8393	0.8797
4	0.2204	0.2995	×	×
5	0.5962	0.6807	0.8664	0.8940
6	0.4452	0.5280	0.8664	0.8940

IRON AND STEEL (1)

Iron and steel (1), as has been already stated, is concerned with the large integrated steel plants. Leontief unit costs of these plants were estimated as follows: the *ASI* 1961, gives the Leontief unit costs for iron and steel (metal) and also the output corresponding to those costs for Bihar and West Bengal. But iron and steel (metal) includes bars and rods, which according to our classification are iron and steel (2) items. Separate output figures for bars and rods are, however, given in the *ASI*. But what posed a serious problem was the splitting of costs into those of iron and steel (1) and bars and rods. It was decided that the only cost item that needed to be excluded from the iron and steel (metal) figures was the cost of rolling billets into bars and rods. Billets, and semi-finished steel in any form according to our classification, were iron and steel (1) items. The *Report of the Tariff Commission on Fair Price Retention of Iron and Steel during 1960*, (1962) provided the plantwise operating charges (Rs./tonne) for bars and rods during 1961–2. From this an average for each of the first two regions was worked out. From the iron and steel (metal) output figures of these two regions the output of bars and rods was subtracted and from their cost figures the corresponding costs of converting billets into bars and rods were deducted.

The *ASI*, 1961, does not provide information on the position of the HSL plant, Bhilai. For this we had to rely on the annual reports of the plant and our correspondence with its production planning department. The annual report of the Bhilai steel plant records information on the value of output produced during the period 1961–2 (we have preferred this year to 1960–1, because in 1961–2 Bhilai was working at optimal capacity). Regarding the cost of raw materials, labour charges, depreciation and other relevant cost items, the problem that confronted us was the estimation of the extent to which the cost of coal increased the raw material cost figures. In our model both coal and iron and steel (1) are endogenous sectors and any flow from one sector to the other is to be determined by the system, and not to be stipulated from outside. From the Hindusthan Steel Plants' *Statistical Report*, published by the Senior Statistical Officer, HSL, Ranchi, we obtained coking and non-coking coal consumption figures for Bhilai in 1961–2. From private correspondence with the production planning department of Bhilai it was learnt that of the total coking coal consumed during 1961–2, 70 per cent was washed and only 30 per cent non-washed. Of the washed coal about 65 per cent came from Kargali at a rate of Rs. 39.82/tonne and 35 per cent from Dugda at a rate of Rs. 49.00/tonne. Non-washed and non-coking coal were, however, valued at Rs. 21.20/tonne. The cost of coal was estimated on the basis of this information and then subtracted from the total cost of raw materials to obtain a meaningful Leontief unit cost.

It was assumed that the hypothetical cost pattern of a steel plant in the south would be similar to that of a steel plant in region 3.

IRON AND STEEL (2)

The iron and steel (2) plants produced a heterogeneous bundle of commodities. The different regions specialized in different sets of products and it was therefore difficult to arrive at a comparable set of cost estimates. Of all the iron and steel (2) items the regions showed comparable product types only in iron and steel castings. We studied the cost differentials in the regions in this group of products. The data necessary for obtaining regional cost estimates were available from the *ASI*. As in the case of other industries, here also two sets of cost estimates were constructed. Also, whenever one member state in a region showed low costs but contributed only a nominal percentage of total regional output, it was not taken into account. The regional differences in costs (in Rs. per Leontief unit) were mainly due to differences in wages. The high cost of Maharastra (0.5962) and low cost of Punjab (0.2204) are largely due to differences in their respective earnings per man-hour.

ENGINEERING (1) AND ENGINEERING (2)

The *ASI* provided the necessary information for constructing these cost coefficients. As in the case of iron and steel (2), here also regional differences in the types of products produced make the comparability of the estimates rather ambiguous. There was also the problem arising from the practice of the *ASI* of recording information in an aggregated form for states having less than three factories. It was difficult on the basis of the available data to divide the aggregated figures amongst the combined states, except by allocating them arbitrarily according to the number of factories in each region. We followed the rule that whenever an industry was found in which the member states of a region had less than three factories, we omitted that industry from its list of engineering (1) or engineering (2), whichever was the case. Of course this was done only for cost and capital-coefficient estimation purposes. This way of tackling heterogeneity in engineering industries gave more or less comparable results for the three dominant producing regions, region 1, region 5 and region 6, but it made the task of estimation impossible for small producers like region 2, for which we had to use the averages of the coefficients of the contiguous regions 1 and 3.

TRANSPORT

The Leontief unit cost in the transportation sector was very roughly estimated from the Railway Board's data on expenses of government railways only.

THE FIXED CAPITAL COEFFICIENT

Some work has been done on the capital structure of the Indian economy under the auspices of the Reserve Bank of India, as well as in a few research centres. Mathur (1965–6), has constructed a 29×29 capital-coefficient matrix for the Indian economy. Attempts at estimation of sectoral coefficients for states or regions, so far as published data indicate, have been rare. An important feature of Dr Mathur's paper is that it suggests outlines for constructing regional coefficients.

Basic data for these coefficients were obtained from the *ASI*, 1960, and the *Reserve Bank of India Bulletin*, 1962. For the coal industry, Ṣanyal's unpublished thesis and the *Official Year Book* of the Calcutta Stock Exchange were once again the main source of information.

Fixed capital in our definition consists of: lands and buildings; plant and machinery; transport equipment. In the *ASI* fixed capital figures (for all industries and states) are the book values of the fixed capital of the plants, and hence they represent the depreciation charges rather than the replacement values of the fixed capital of the plants in which we are interested. Mathur resolved this difficulty by inflating the book value so as to represent the original cost, by using company accounts data for the year 1960 analysed by the Reserve Bank of India (vol. 16 (1962), pp. 1,160–78). However, he did not correct for price changes between the installation year and 1960. The reason in his words was that 'most fixed capital in 1960 would be comparatively recent vintage and hence absence of this correction may not materially affect this result.' In working out our set of regional fixed capital coefficients we accepted this principle.

When calculating the ratio between the original value of fixed capital and its depreciated value in 1960 from the table in the *Reserve Bank of India Bulletin*, 1962 (pp. 1160–78), the value of land was omitted from both sides. For iron and steel (1) and iron and steel (2) the same index was adopted as was obtained for the base metal group; for engineering (1) and engineering (2) we applied the index obtained for the group made up of transport equipment, electrical equipment and non-electrical equipment.

Using these ratios we inflated the depreciated book value of 1960 fixed capital in iron and steel (1), iron and steel (2), engineering (1) and engineering (2) to their respective replacement values in 1960. The output of those industries in 1960 was also calculated from the *ASI*, 1960. The ratio of the former to the latter gave us the fixed capital coefficients for these four groups.

The fixed capital coefficients of the coal industry was obtained in a different way. Average gross amounts of capital in the coal industry in different regions during 1960 were obtained from the *Official Year Book* of the Calcutta Stock Exchange, 1962. The aim was to find the average fixed capital coefficients for firms earning normal profits. This limited the number of firms eligible for inclusion. The corresponding output (in money terms) of the representative collieries was in some cases obtained from Sanyal's thesis (1964). In all other cases the corresponding raisings (in tonnes), shown in the *Official Year Book* of Calcutta Stock Exchange, were valued at the prices assumed to be prevailing during that period.

The fixed capital coefficient in coal for region 6 was based on information available for the most important group of collieries there, Singareni. This group of collieries saw a good deal of new investment in the early sixties, when its fixed capital amounted to about Rs. 6 crores and its annual capacity was increased to about 3 million tonnes. Granting a higher price,

Rs. 28.05/tonne, for Singareni coal (Rangrez *et al.*, 1961), we arrive at a fixed capital coefficient of 0.7130 for region 6.

The capital/output ratio of the transportation sector is based on capital at charge and gross earnings of the government railways.

TABLE A6–9.3. *Gross fixed capital/output ratios*

Region	Capital/output ratio of		
	Iron and steel (2)	Engineering (1)	Engineering (2)
1	0.3752	0.5446	0.4396
2	0.9043	1.3029	0.4057
3	0.6846	0.9016	6.1898
4	0.9876	0.2681	0.1576
5	0.4112	0.4303	0.9272
6	1.0441	0.5572	0.9785

Capital /output ratio of Iron and steel (1)	
Bhilai	5.1583
Durgapur	5.0743
Rourkela	5.5688
TISCO	1.6746
IISCO	1.6091

Region	Capital/output ratio of Coal
1	1.2277
2	0.6014
3	0.5896
4	×
5	0.6346†
6	0.7130

Region	Capital/output ratio of Transport
1	4.9120
2	3.8984
3	3.3282
4	3.3596
5	2.6985
6	2.9872

† Based on data of a single company – Amalgamated Coal.
B. Sanyal: 'Cost of Production of Coal in India', unpublished Ph.D. dissertation at Jadavpur University, Calcutta, 1964.

REGIONAL PROFIT RATES

The *ASI* was the main source used for the estimation of profit in the iron and steel and engineering sectors. Profit was defined as the value added by manufacture less salaries, wages, benefits, privileges and rent. We felt that the profit figures thus measured would be less liable to under-estimation.

For iron and steel (1), iron and steel (2), engineering (1) and engineering (2), regional profits for 1960 were calculated from the *ASI* for that year.

Profit rates in coal were computed from the *Official Year Book* of the Calcutta Stock Exchange, 1962. For the other industries we worked with profits after depreciation but before taxation. Accordingly, while collecting profit figures from the Stock Exchange *Year Book*, taxes were added to net profits. These profit rates were based on a limited number of collieries in each state, particularly for region 3 and region 5. We therefore pooled together the data for collieries in Madhya Pradesh and Maharastra. The profit rate obtained was assumed to be valid for both region 3 and region 5. No information was available on the profit rates of south Indian collieries. We therefore had to satisfy ourselves with the average profit rate obtaining in central Indian coalfields as representative of that prevailing in coal mines in region 6.

TABLE A6–9.4. *The regional profit rate of fixed capital*

Region	Coal	Engineering (1)	Engineering (2)	Iron and steel (1)	Iron and steel (2)	Transport
1	0.1252	0.6285	0.4744	0.1201	0.2299	0.6866
2	0.0934	0.1266	0.3873	0.0490	0.2590	0.5458
3	0.0921	0.5776	0.1793	—	0.1977	0.4668
4	—	0.5673	0.1090	—	0.4131	0.4708
5	—	0.3780	0.3165	—	0.3393	0.3785
6	—	0.4946	0.3696	—	0.1634	0.4183

INTERREGIONAL TRANSPORTATION COSTS

It has already been pointed out that regional production and consumption are assumed to take place at a central point in the region. These points are Calcutta for region 1, Jamshedpur for region 2, Bhopal for region, 3, Jullundhur for region 4, Bombay for region 5 and Bangalore for region 6. All foreign exports and imports are assumed to pass through one of the three ports Calcutta, Bombay and Madras. For exports and imports a transportation cost is involved only in the transit of merchandise from the centres of production to the ports or from the ports to the centres of consumption. All transportation costs are rail transportation costs of average Leontief units.

In estimating interregional transportation costs no distinction was made between iron and steel (1) and iron and steel (2). In other words it was assumed that all categories of iron and steel output had the same freight rate. Given the regional Leontief units, the freight rates and the rail distance between the seven representative points, the transportation charge for Re 1 worth of merchandise is easily computed. The shortest rail distances between any pair of these seven points were considered. Zonewise freight rates for coal and iron and steel are available in the Railway Board *Annual Reports*. The *Annual Report* for 1960–1 not being available, we had to depend on that for 1959–60. But it was noted that there was a 5 per cent increase in the levy over the 1959–60 freight rate and the 1959–60 freight rates were inflated accordingly.

The Railway Board charges different freight rates for different consumers of coal. For example, it has one rate for steel plants, another rate for ports and yet another rate for government consumption. We used the freight rate under the heading 'coal for the public'. Similarly for iron and steel the freight rate charged for 'Iron and steel wrought' was used. The all-India average for broad gauge lines was accepted as the relevant rate.

The report of the Railway Board does not show a freight rate for engineering goods. It records the rate for a blanket category, 'other revenue-earning commodities'. But that obviously cannot be representative of the freight rate on the engineering type of goods. Das & Sardesai (1965–6), have however, given an estimate of freight rates in what they call 'heavy basic industries'. Their definition of 'heavy basic industries' encompasses metal and metal products as well as our engineering industries. In the absence of better data it was adopted for engineering (1) and engineering (2).

TABLE A6–9.5. *Freight rates for shipment of Re 1 worth of merchandise (in Rs.)*

	Calcutta	Jamshed-pur	Bhopal	Jullun-dhur	Bombay	Banga-lore	Madras
			Coal				
Calcutta	—	0.2226	1.3441	1.5579	1.7539	1.7892	1.4776
Jamshedpur	0.2621	—	1.3318	1.8351	1.8037	2.0761	1.7615
Bhopal	1.5347	1.2910	—	1.0877	0.8540	1.6976	1.5043
Jullundhur							
Bombay	2.0026	1.7485	0.8540	1.7789	—	1.1281	1.3010
Bangalore	1.5312	1.5084	1.2723	2.0876	0.8455	—	0.2741
Madras	1.2645	1.2798	1.1275	1.9427	0.9751	0.2741	—
			Iron and steel (1)				
Calcutta	—	0.0396	0.2391	0.2771	0.3119	0.3183	0.2628
Jamshedpur	0.0259	—	0.1315	0.1812	0.1781	0.2050	0.1739
Bhopal	0.1287	0.1083	—	0.0912	0.0716	0.1424	0.1262
Bombay	0.2279	0.1990	0.0972	0.2025	—	0.1284	0.1481
Madras	0.1921	0.1944	0.1712	0.2951	0.1481	0.0416	—
			Iron and steel (2)				
Calcutta	—	0.0335	0.2023	0.2345	0.2639	0.2693	0.2224
Jamshedpur	0.0107	—	0.0541	0.0746	0.0733	0.0844	0.0716
Bhopal	0.0552	0.0464	—	0.0391	0.0307	0.0610	0.0541
Jullundhur	0.1812	0.1812	0.1108	—	0.1812	0.2837	0.2640
Bombay	0.0600	0.0524	0.0256	0.0533	—	0.0338	0.0390
Bangalore	0.1102	0.1085	0.0915	0.1502	0.0608	—	0.0197
Madras	0.0910	0.0921	0.0811	0.1398	0.0702	0.0197	—
			Engineering (1) and Engineering (2)				
Calcutta	—	0.0125	0.0755	0.0875	0.0985	0.1005	0.0830
Jamshedpur	0.0125	—	0.0635	0.0875	0.0860	0.0990	0.0840
Bhopal	0.0755	0.0635	—	0.0535	0.0420	0.0835	0.0740
Jullundhur	0.0875	0.0785	0.0535	—	0.0875	0.1370	0.1275
Bombay	0.0985	0.0860	0.0420	0.0875	—	0.0555	0.0640
Bangalore	0.1005	0.0990	0·0835	0.1370	0.0555	—	0.0180
Madras	0.0830	0.0840	0.0740	0.1275	0.0640	0.0180	—

REGIONAL FINAL DEMAND

Final demand in input–output studies includes household consumption, government consumption, stocks, gross fixed capital formation, export and import. But our stipulated final demand also includes intermediate consumption of the output of the endogenous sectors (i.e. coal, iron and steel, engineering and transport) by the residual sectors. For example, final demand for coal in any region, according to our definition, is the sum total of that region's household and government consumption of coal, the addition made to its stock in that year, its export from the region during the period and the coal consumed by all the producing sectors in the economy except the endogenous sectors less the import of coal into that region.

Manne and Rudra (1965) have worked out an inter-industry transaction matrix for 1960–1 for India. This table, after appropriate modifications for price charges (their figures are at 1959–69 produces' prices) and sectoral coverage, served as our basic source for all-India final demand. The different components of this all-India final demand were then distributed amongst the regions.

A regional breakdown of government expenditure was made on the basis of public employment. The *Census of Central Goverment Employees* (1965) showed the distribution of central government employees by states and pay-ranges for 1964. The structure underlying the 1964–5 situation was assumed to be valid for the whole period 1960–5 and a distribution of central and quasi-government employees for 1960–1 over regions and pay ranges was effected. Following the same principle and utilising information on the distribution of pay-ranges between the different states provided by the *Census of Central Government Employees*, 1961, we worked out the regional salary bills of state and local government employees. Adding the salary bill of central and quasi-government employees to that of the state and local government employees we obtained regional earnings from public employment. As no breakdown of the pay ranges of Orissa and Madras state government employees was available, we used the break-down of the contiguous states in their cases (Bihar in the case of Orissa and Mysore for Madras). Similarly no information on the pay-scale of local government employees being available, we split them up in the ratio of the respective state government employees.

GROSS FIXED CAPITAL FORMATION

Of the endogenous sectors only engineering and iron and steel contribute directly to capital formation. The contribution of the engineering industry to gross fixed capital formation is explicitly mentioned in Manne & Rudra (1965). The contribution of iron and steel under that head is not given. Here again the procedure the authors adopt is to inflate the flow from iron and steel to construction by the ratio of the value of urban constructional output to the value of materials consumed for that purpose, and to show the result as the contribution o urban construction towards capital formation. The flow of iron and steel to construction is accepted here as an indicator of capital formation in the iron and steel sector.

Regarding the regional division of aggregate capital formation in any sector of the economy, Professor Leontief's suggestion is to break it up according to the share of each region in national construction activity. No firm data exist on regional construction activity. Our method of forming an index of regional construction activity was as follows.

The following function was assumed for the Indian economy

$$Y = a + bX + cZ,$$

where Y denotes construction activity, X denotes cement consumption in construction and Z finished steel consumption in construction.

The term 'construction' includes the following activities which are purely constructional activities: minor irrigation; irrigation and flood-control schemes; hydro-electric power; roads and bridges for roads; housing and the constructional part of such ventures as railways and communication, schools, colleges and hospitals etc.

A curve was fitted with Indian data for the period 1951–2 to 1960–1. The fit obtained was

$$Y = -466\,0000 + 3221X + 0433Z \quad (r_{YXZ} = 0.975),$$

and the original and the estimated values agreed well.

Making the reasonable assumption that cement is consumed only by construction activities, we equated the cement received by the regions during 1960–1 (Manne, 1967) with cement consumption in construction by those regions in 1960–1. The estimation of regional finished steel consumption in construction was more complicated. Figures for finished steel consumption during 1960–1 by the regions (i.e. production plus import less export) were obtained from Johnson (1967). But these figures included the industrial demand for finished steel. An estimate was made from the *ASI* (1960) of finished steel consumption (regionwise) in the main consuming industries: iron and steel, metal products and engineering. Regional finished steel consumption by the construction sector was then easily derived. Once these regional figures of cement and finished steel consumption were obtained they were applied to the '*b*' and '*c*' coefficients and summed regionwise. This provided us with an index of regional construction activity.

TABLE A6–9.6. *Regional construction activity (at 1960–1 prices)*

Region	Construction (Rs. crores)	Percentage distribution
1	200.2972	12.61
2	195.3732	12.30
3	275.9051	17.37
4	190.9257	12.02
5	338.0115	21.28
6	387.8873	24.42
Total	1588.4000	100.00

STOCKS AND EXPORTS

Data on additions to stocks or inventory accumulation were available for all sectors except transportation, where the question of addition to stocks does not arise. For each sector the share of the regions in its net addition to stocks was based on the share of the regions in national income.

Exports were arbitrarily allocated on the basis of 1960–1 actual production. The only thing that can be said in defence of such a crude method is that the exports of commodities in which we are interested were so insignificant that the resulting error is not likely to affect the broad pattern of our optimal solutions.

INTERMEDIATE CONSUMPTION OF THE PRODUCTS OF THE ENDOGENOUS SECTORS BY THE REMAINING PRODUCING SECTORS OF THE ECONOMY

Since our models are in the nature of partial equilibrium models, the intermediate consumption of the products of the endogenous sectors by residual sectors has to be stipulated exogenously. After appropriate price changes the inter-industry transaction table of Manne & Rudra (1965) provided us with the necessary data. In this table there is a column headed 'others'. This was added to the appropriate sub-total of intermediate consumption. The next problem was to find the share of the regions.

It was noted that only non-electrical equipment and coal were consumed in significant quantities as intermediate input by other sectors of the economy. For non-electrical equipment the important consumers were construction, iron and ore mining, other minerals, food industries, jute textiles, glass, wooden and other non-metallic products, petroleum products, rubber products and the chemical industry. For coal the dominant users were cement, other metals, plantations, leather and leather products, food grains and food industries, cotton textiles, jute textiles, chemical fertilisers, glass, wooden and other non-metallic products, rubber products, the chemical industry, electricity and others. The partial equilibrium nature of our models permitted us to use the 1960–1 outputs of these consuming sectors, as given. Once the regional outputs of these consuming industries were known, the regional distribution of the intermediate inputs followed.

IMPORTS

Imports were classified into two groups – maintenance imports and project imports. Maintenance imports for iron and steel and engineering for 1964–5 were obtained from Table BP. 2.1, in Perspective Planning Division's (1966) *Draft Fourth Plan, Material and Financial Balances*. Subtracting these from the corresponding total imports (see Inter-industrial flows and pattern of final demand, 1964–5, *ibid.*), the project imports of these two items were obtained as a residual. For these two groups the ratio of maintenance imports to project imports was observed. The actual division of iron and steel imports into those of iron and steel (1) and iron and steel (2) and of engineering imports into engineering (1) and engineering (2) were noted. Imports in each of these four items were then broken down into maintenance imports and project imports, using the ratio constructed before. Project imports were distributed amongst regions in the ratio of their construction activities and maintenance imports in the ratio of their industrial production.

TABLE A6–9.7. *Regional imports (in Rs.)*

Region	Project imports		Maintenance imports	
	Engineering (1)	Engineering (2)	Engineering (1)	Engineering (2)
1	15.05	9.89	19.83	13.03
2	14.68	9.65	6.91	4.54
3	20.73	13.63	8.12	5.34
4	14.35	9.43	3.44	2.26
5	25.40	16.19	25.74	16.92
6	29.14	19.15	12.27	8.06

Region	Project imports		Maintenance imports	
	Iron and steel (1)	Iron and steel (2)	Iron and steel (1)	Iron and steel (2)
1	0.92	0.74	15.27	12.27
2	0.89	0.72	5.32	4.27
3	1.26	1.01	6.25	5.03
4	0.87	0.70	2.65	2.13
5	1.54	1.24	9.82	15.93
6	1.78	1.43	9.45	7.59

TABLE A6–9.8. *Regional exports*

Region	Engineering (1)	Engineering (2)	Iron and steel (1)	Iron and steel (2)	Coal
1	0.82	0.41	1.67	0.16	
2			1.67	0.16	0.60
3			1.68		0.60
4					
5	0.82	0.41		0.16	
6	0.81	0.41			0.60

TABLE A6–9.9. *Components of final demand (in crores of Rs.) by region*

Region	Household consumption	Govt consumption	Gross fixed capital formation	Non-endogenous industrial consumption	Stocks	Exports	Imports
			Iron and steel (1)				
1	×	×	9.3909	0.4962	—	1.6700	16.1900
2	×	×	9.1601	0.5614	—	1.6700	6.2100
3	×	×	12.9358	0.9641	—	1.6800	7.5100
4	×	×	8.9515	0.2821	—	—	3.5200
5	×	×	15.8476	0.9705	—	—	21.3600
6	×	×	18.1861	1.1429	—	—	11.2300
			Iron and steel (2)				
1	×	×	22.9915	—	—	0.1600	13.0100
2	×	×	22.4263	—	—	0.1600	4.9900
3	×	×	31.6704	—	—	—	6.0400
4	×	×	21.9158	—	—	—	2.8300
5	×	×	38.7994	—	—	0.1600	17.1700
6	×	×	44.5245	—	—	—	9.0200
			Coal				
1	0.7351	×	—	0.2654	7.6719	—	—
2	0.3904	×	—	0.2468	4.1924	0.6000	—
3	1.0968	×	—	0.5157	6.9157	0.6000	—
4	0.5472	×	—	0.1509	11.0755	—	—
5	1.5360	×	—	0.5191	18.3548	—	—
6	1.7946	×	—	0.6113	7.2998	0.6000	—
			Transport				
1	34.7002	×	—	—	83.8560	—	—
2	14.9858	×	—	—	75.3650	—	—
3	13.7759	×	—	—	135.9131	—	—
4	13.7759	×	—	—	31.7075	—	—
5	46.5896	×	—	—	125.4491	—	—
6	38.2193	×	—	—	97.9194	—	—

CAPACITY

The models in this study are optimisation models, operating under exogenously assigned final demands and regional capacities. The capacity estimates are admittedly very uncertain. Organised capacity data are available only for a limited number of industries, like iron and steel (base metal) and some important branches of engineering. No published data, of the coal-raising capacities of collieries are available. The coal capacity estimates are therefore subject to a wide margin of error. The same may be said of our transport capacity estimates. There are several limiting factors in rail transport capacity, e.g. line capacity, engine availability, lack of block signal facilities, shortage of wagons and coaches, etc. It is not possible to acquire enough information about each of these factors for all the railway zones in all the regions from the published statistical information. The bottleneck factors in road transport are still more evasive. The transport capacity estimates are therefore also of a tentative nature.

Complete and more-or less firm data exist only for our classification of iron and steel (1). These are taken from *Hindusthan Steel Statistics* published by the Senior Statistical Officer, HSL, Ranchi. There are five major steel plants for which itemwise finished and semi-finished steel capacity are given. The figures are in tonnes. To express them in money values 1961 *ASI* prices were used for the states in which these plants are located.

Iron and steel (2) capacity estimates are not so straightforward. Regional capacities in structurals, castings and forgings and pipes and tubes may be arrived at by multiplying 1961 regional production in these branches by the corresponding under-utilization factor during the period. The estimates are inaccurate as they utilize the same all-India under-utilisation factor for all the regions. The prices used are *ASI* prices for 1961.

The re-rolling capacity of billet and scrap re-rollers and secondary producers was estimated by a committee appointed by the government in July 1956 at 7 lakhs tonnes on a single shift basis by the end of April 1957 (Planning Commission, 1962). Though the government sanctioned a few additional re-rolling units in states where very little capacity was currently available, it can be safely assumed that these new units could not start production before the end of 1960–1. So for our purposes in 1960–1 billet and scrap re-rollers had an annual capacity of 7,19,000 tonnes (according to iron and steel controller) of rolled products, mainly bars and rods. In rupees this amounted to about 4020 lakhs valued at Rs. 551 per tonne. This capacity, it was assumed was shared by the regions in the proportion to their respective finished steel production during the period by their re-rolling units.

Since organised capacity data are available only for the principal engineering industries, we could not depend on them. Instead, as in the case of some of the iron and steel (2) items, we used the under-utilisation factor. Under-utilisation percentages were known for such classifications as transport equipment, electrical equipment and non-electrical equipment, rather than for engineering (1) and engineering (2). Therefore 1961 *ASI* output figures for all our engineering industries in all the regions were collected, the broad class (i.e. whether transport or electrical or non-electrical equipment) observed, the appropriate under-utilisation factor applied and the figures finally rearranged into engineering (1) and engineering (2) categories.

TABLE A6–9.10. *Capacities by sector and region (in crores of Rs.)*

Region	Iron and steel (1)	Iron and steel (2)	Engineering (1)	Engineering (2)
1	90.46	87.29	114.24	197.03
2	149.78	16.89	15.14	9.87
3	40.89	7.14	29.59	15.30
4	—	9.24	16.83	15.42
5	—	54.51	130.05	117.96
6	—	8.62	102.36	49.08

TABLE A6–9.11. *Capital-output ratios and profit rates*

Region	Coal		Iron and steel (1)		Iron and steel (2)		Engineering (1)		Engineering (2)		Transport	
	Capital-output ratio	Profit rate	Capital-output ratio	Profit rate	Capital-output ratio	Profit rate	Capital-output ratio	Profit rate	Capital-output ratio	Profit rate	Capital-output ratio	Profit rate
1	1.2277	0.1537	5.0743	0.6094	0.3752	0.0868	0.5446	0.3423	0.4396	0.2085	11.90	0.6866
2	0.0614	0.0562	5.5688	0.2729	0.9043	0.2343	1.3029	—	0.4057	0.1571	9.46	0.5458
3	0.5896	0.0543	5.1583	0.2528	0.6846	0.1353	0.9016	0.5208	0.5817	0.1043	8.09	0.4668
4	—	—	—	—	0.9876	0.4080	0.2681	—	0.1576	0.0172	8.16	0.4708
5	0.6346	0.0584	—	—	0.4112	0.1395	0.4303	—	0.9272	0.2935	6.56	0.3785
6	0.7130	0.1241	—	—	1.0441	0.1706	0.5572	0.2756	0.9756	0.3617	7.25	0.4183

TABLE A6–9.12. *Final demand (in crores of Rs.)*

Region	1961†	1971	1975
		Coal	
1	9.27	26.66	38.91
2	5.42	15.06	22.43
3	9.13	25.45	37.54
4	1.77	4.65	6.79
5	20.41	61.40	87.89
6	9.61	27.37	39.65
		Iron and steel (1)	
1	11.55	14.94	140.07
2	11.29	26.72	142.92
3	15.58	38.03	198.44
4	9.23	19.35	113.92
5	16.81	16.79	198.31
6	19.32	36.39	236.78
		Iron and steel (2)	
1	10.14	38.95	111.09
2	17.60	47.51	113.01
3	25.63	68.22	158.39
4	19.08	48.62	110.04
5	21.79	71.14	188.83
6	35.50	94.03	220.62
		Engineering (1)	
1	57.90	101.99	201.74
2	65.09	107.36	189.78
3	106.75	172.52	300.84
4	59.42	104.87	177.96
5	110.02	195.63	361.40
6	136.38	226.66	404.74
		Engineering (2)	
1	29.61	52.40	109.41
2	35.22	57.89	105.57
3	58.01	93.59	167.74
4	31.71	56.31	98.08
5	59.12	105.71	201.66
6	74.05	122.51	224.80
		Transport	
1	99.84	279.81	427.85
2	70.46	183.36	279.44
3	118.92	307.98	470.40
4	33.61	92.25	137.53
5	117.05	327.06	501.82
6	102.36	274.76	419.75

† The figures for 1961 final demand treat foreign imports in the iron and steel (1) sector as variables of the system. Total foreign imports are, however, restricted to a value of Rs. 66.02 crores.

TABLE A6–9.12 (*cont.*)

Region	1971
	Overhead
1	1074.20
2	398.40
3	485.50
4	267.40
5	1550.10
6	787.60

TABLE A6–9.13. *Excess capacity in model 1 (in crores of Rs.)*

Sector	Region	1971	1975
Coal	1	35.447	220.00
	2	0	29.51
	3	0	0
	5	0	0
	6	0	0
Iron and steel (1)	1	255.301	804.50
	2	0	0
	3	101.855	60.29
	4	0	0
Iron and steel (2)	1	88.834	207.61
	2	37.602	87.88
	3	37.317	99.04
	4	286.804	670.28
	5	45.225	105.95
	6	257.390	286.60
Engineering (1)	1	84.12	145.31
	2	164.383	285.97
	3	93.42	167.37
	4	0	0
	5	512.486	981.95
	6	255.302	333.14
Engineering (2)	1	22.03	37.10
	2	34.12	57.48
	3	0	0
	4	0	0
	5	0	0
	6	0	0
Transport	1	×	×
	2	×	×
	3	×	×
	4	×	×
	5	×	×

× Indicates capacity not provided for.

TABLE A6–9.14. *Excess capacity in model 3 (in crores of Rs.)*

Sector	Region	1961	1971	1975
Coal	1	1.24	37.41	244.26
	2		0	0
	3		0	0
	5		0	0
	6		0	0
Iron and steel (1)	1	7	257.44	804.50
	2		95.83	16.76
	3		0	0
Iron and steel (2)	1	70	277.17	659.91
	2	28	88.83	207.61
	3	39	37.60	87.88
	4		48.62	113.63
	5		0	0
	6	63	45.34	105.95
Engineering (1)	1	175	0	0
	2	72	84.12	145.31
	3	39	164.38	283.97
	4	45	93.42	161.37
	5	245	242.55	327.75
	6	136	568.43	981.95
Engineering (2)	1		266.37	343.28
	2	21	22.03	37.10
	3	8	34.12	57.48
	4		0	0
	5	48	0	0
	6	27	0	0
Transport	1	33	×	×
	2	9	×	×
	3	5	×	×
	4	11	×	×
	5	8	×	×
	6	30	×	×

TABLE A6–9.15. *Utilisation of capacity in different models (in crores of Rs.)*

| Sector | Region | Excess capacity 1971 | |
		Model 4	Model 5
Coal	1	0	0
	2	0	0
	3	0	0
	5	0	0
	6	0	0
Iron and steel (1)	1	0	0
	2	209.99	0
	3	116.32	0
Iron and steel (2)	1	457.12	0
	2	30.13	88.83
	3	0	0
	4	0	0
	5	0	2.13
	6	0	0
Engineering (1)	1	0	0
	2	84.12	84.12
	3	0	0
	4	93.42	93.42
	5	722.38	722.38
	6	295.88	94.99
Engineering (2)	1	209.07	137.54
	2	22.03	22.03
	3	34.12	34.12
	4	34.40	34.40
	5	0	0
	6	0	0
Transport	1	0	1534.59
	2	0	15.16
	3	0	0
	4	0	0
	5	0	0
	6	0	0

TABLE A6–9.16. *Utilisation of capacity*

Sector	Region	Excess capacity model 4 (1975)
Coal	1	0
	2	0
	3	0
	5	0
	6	0
Iron and steel (1)	1	0
	2	0
	3	64.27

TABLE A6–9.16 (*cont.*)

Sector	Region	Excess capacity model 4 (1975)
Iron and steel (2)	1	582.37
	2	207.61
	3	87.88
	4	0
	5	237.62
	6	0
Engineering (1)	1	0
	2	145.31
	3	0
	4	161.37
	5	1247.90
	6	421.27
Engineering (2)	1	0
	2	0
	3	0
	4	0
	5	0
	6	0
Transport	1	0
	2	0
	3	0
	4	0
	5	0
	6	0

REFERENCES

Bellman, R. E. & Dreyfus, S. E. [1962]. *Applied Dynamic Programming*. Princeton, New Jersey.

Das, N. and Sardesai, D. B. [1965–6]. Location of industries in India: transport cost minimisation. *Artha Vijnana*, vol. 9, nos. 3 and 4.

Dhar, R. [1965]. Inter-regional input–output analysis of the Indian economy (1953–4). Unpublished thesis, submitted at Jadavpur University, Calcutta.

Doig, A. G. and Land, A. H. [1960]. An automatic method for solving discrete programming problems. *Econometrica*, vol. 28. no. 3.

Frisch, R. [1957]. *Oslo Channel Model*. Oslo Decision Models, University Institute of Economics, Oslo.

Ghosh, A. [1965]. *Efficiency in Location and Inter-regional Flows: the Indian Current Industry during the Five Year Plans, 1950–9*. Amsterdam.

Ghosh, A. [1968]. Inter-regional models and the problem of substitution. In *Planning, Programming and Input–output Models: Selected Papers on Indian Planning*. Cambridge.

Gomory, R. E. [1963]. An algorithm for integer solutions to linear professors. In *Recent Advances in Mathematical Programming*, ed. R. L. Graves and P. Wolfe. New York.

Isard, W. [1953]. Inter-regional analysis and regional development. *American Economic Review*, vol. 43.

Johnson, W. A. [1967]. *The Steel Industry of India*. Harvard University Press.

Kurz, M. [1965]. Optimal paths of capital accumulation under the minimum time objective. *Econometrica*, vol. 33, no. 1.

Leontief, W. [1953]. Inter-regional theory. In *Studies in the Structure of the American Economy*, by Leontief and others. New York.

Leontief, W. & Strout, A. [1963]. Multiregional input–output analysis. In *Structural Interdependence and Economic Development*, ed. T. Barna. New York.

Manne, A. S. [1967]. *Investment for Capacity Expansion*. London.

Manne, A. S. & Rudra, A. [1965]. A consistency model of India's Fourth Plan. *Sankhya*, vol. 27, parts I and II.

Mathur, P. N. [1965–6]. An inter-industry capital table for India – first approximation (1960). *Artha Vijnana*, vol. 9, nos. 3 and 4.

Moses, L. N. [1955]. The stability of inter-regional trading patterns and input–output analysis. *American Economic Review*, vol. 14.

Perspective Planning Division, Planning Commission, Govt of India. [1966]. *Draft Fourth Plan, Material and Financial Balances 1964–5, 1970–1 and 1975–6*.

Planning Commission, Govt of India. [1960] *Programmes of Industrial Development, 1961–6*.

Rangrez, K. G. *et al.* [1961]. *A study of the Economics of Low Temperature Carbonisation Industry in India*, Seminar Volume on Low Temperature Carbonisation of Non-coking Coal.

Roy, A. [1968]. *Iron and Steel Review*, vol. 9, no. 1.

Sanyal, B. [1964]. Cost of production of coal in India. Unpublished doctoral dissertation submitted at Jadavpur University, Calcutta.

Tariff Commission, Govt of India [1962]. *Report of the Tariff Commission on Fair Price Retention of Iron and Steel during 1960*.

INDEX

Accounting relation, *see* Balance relation
Asymmetric dual, *see* Dual, asymmetric

Balance relation, 10, 18–22, 50, 74
Bellman, R. E., 61, 101

Capacity
  constraints, 19–21, 25, 27–30
  estimates, 94, 97–8
  utilisation, 15, 33–5, 37–8, 56–8, 99–100
  see also Overhead facilities, utilisation of
Capital
  accumulation, 35–8, 64–72; *see also* Gross
    fixed capital formation *and* Investment
  coefficient, fixed, *see* Fixed capital coefficient
  concept of, 21–2
  cost, 21–2, 57–9; minimisation of, 21–2,
    35–9, 43, 45–7, 54–6, 61–2
  utilisation, 21, 37–42, 52, 56–8; *see also*
    Overhead facilities, utilisation of
Capital–output ratios, 21, 37, 41, 45, 55,
  62–7, 95
Cement industry in India, 1, 11–17, 25–9,
  73–6
Coal industry in India, 25–9, 31–45, 52–9,
  73–80, 82–9, 92–9
Coefficients
  fixed capital, *see* Fixed capital coefficients
  input–output, *see* Input–output coefficients
  inter–industry input coefficients, *see* Inter–
    industry input coefficients
  Leontief coefficients, *see* Leontief
  production coefficients, *see* Production
  region, *see* Regional coefficients
Commodities
  interregional flows of, *see* Interregional
    flows
  national, *see* National Commodities
  regional, *see* Regional commodities
  see also Cement, Coal, Cotton, Iron and
    steel, Jute *and* Sugar
Competition, perfect, *see* Perfect competition
Constant of attraction, *see* Leontief gravity
  model
Constraints
  in profit-maximising model, 39, 58–9
  on capacity, *see* Capacity constraints
  system of linear programming model,
    18–19

Consumption
  government, 93
  household, 93
  intermediate, 91–2
  see also Final demand
Costs
  capital, *see* Capital costs
  labour, *see* Labour costs
  of final output, *see* Final output
  overhead, *see* Overhead costs
  transport, *see* Transport costs
Cotton industry in India, 25–9, 73–6

Das, N., 89, 101
Demand, final, *see* Final demand
Dhar, R., 25, 78, 101
Doig, A. G., 61, 101
Dreyfus, S. E., 61, 101
Dual formulation (of linear programming
  models), 2, 48–59
  asymmetric dual, 49–50
  basic model, 48–9
  dual solutions, 2, 58
  see also Implicit prices, Rent, *and* Shadow
    variables
Dynamic programming, 61–2

Energy production, 7; *see also* Coal
Engineering industry in India, 31–4, 36–8,
  40–5, 52–9, 77–9, 81–90, 92–100
Exports (from India), 91, 93

Final demand, 8–9, 22, 55–6, 59, 74, 76
  regional, 90, 93, 96–7
Final output, cost of, 57–9
Fixed capital coefficients, 86–7
Fixed capital formation, *see* Gross fixed
  capital formation
Fixed coefficient approach to interregional
  problems, 1, 4–10
Fixed coefficient models, 4–5, 18
  application of, 11–17
  linear programming model, *see* Linear
    programming
  of Isard, *see* Isard
  of Leontief, *see* Leontief
  price-influenced substitution model, *see*
    Price-influenced substitution model
  regression models, *see* Regression models
Frisch, R., 7, 101